W9-CPB-600

Leadership Matters:
Police Chiefs Talk About Their Careers

Edited by Craig Fischer

POLICE EXECUTIVE
RESEARCH FORUM

Police Executive Research Forum, Washington, D.C. 20036
Copyright 2009 by Police Executive Research Forum

All rights reserved

Printed in the United States of America

ISBN: 978-1-934485-09-5

Cover and interior design by Dave Williams

Contents

Acknowledgments

Many talented people contributed to this book in a variety of ways, and I would like to thank all of them for offering their time and expertise. So often, the Police Executive Research Forum calls on its members and friends to help us with a major project, and the strong response that we receive is humbling and inspiring. This book is a prime example of that generosity of spirit.

Perhaps the best way to approach this is chronologically. I'll start by thanking Chief Bob McNeilly, who helped provide the vision for writing this book. I have known Bob since he first started as chief of the Pittsburgh Bureau of Police. He took over the department when it was grappling with a U.S. Justice Department consent decree, and he courageously transformed the department and made it a model for others to visit and learn from. For example, Bob is credited with developing the first early warning system to track officer performance.

Over the years, Bob and I had talked about the challenges that face police chiefs across the country, and it occurred to us that someone ought to tap into the depth of experience of chiefs who have been around the block a few times, and who could offer sound advice to their colleagues about how to recognize opportunities and avoid the pitfalls of the job.

So Bob arranged a meeting for us with the Scaife Foundations, which are based in Pittsburgh. The people at Scaife were very supportive, and kindly provided PERF with funding to get this project up and running. In particular, I would like to thank Michael Gleba, Executive Vice President of the Sarah Scaife Foundation, who immediately saw the need for this work and enthusiastically supported it.

Next, we contacted two criminal justice veterans, Barbara McDonald and Gwen Holden, who agreed to conduct the research for this book. Barbara has extensive experience in the Chicago Police Department, and Gwen for many years served as executive director of the National Criminal Justice Association. They worked with PERF to develop a plan for selecting experienced chiefs who would be interviewed. They came up with good questions and set about interviewing the chiefs, using their own expertise to explore the issues and to zero in on the really useful information, the kinds of facts and analyses that are timeless. Barbara and Gwen never lost sight of their target—helping experienced chiefs to provide guidance not only to new chiefs who are just starting out, but also to experienced chiefs who can learn by hearing about how their colleagues have managed the job of police chief. When the interviewing was done, Gwen and Barbara painstakingly organized all of the chiefs' stories and remarks and wrote the first draft of this book.

Now would be a good time to offer PERF's thanks to the people at the heart of this book—the chiefs who provided the stories, the examples of what they have faced, and the hard-headed analysis that makes this book not a mere collection of stories, but rather a practical guide to being an effective chief. All of the 25 chiefs in this book are very smart, hard-working, and ambitious. Some are funny. And a few might be described as "characters." They by no means have perfect records; in fact, many of these chiefs will be the first to tell you they have made some missteps along the way. But they have learned and emerged stronger because of the lessons they learned.

I believe that readers of this book will come away with a better appreciation of the job of police chief. The chiefs interviewed for this book provide a cross-section of chiefs' experiences from departments, both small and large. Some moved up through the ranks within a police department to the top job, while others came from outside. They all agreed to tell their stories so others can learn from their successes as well as the challenges they have faced. I am very grateful to all of the chiefs who contributed to this book.

Finally, there are some people at PERF who helped to shepherd this project along. Our Director of Homeland Security and Development, Jerry Murphy, provided overall management of the project and worked tirelessly to keep the book on track. Charlotte Lansinger, our executive search guru, provided valuable comments and suggestions. Craig Fischer took the initial draft, and as I have seen him do on a number of occasions, expertly edited and organized it to make the final version a very readable and enjoyable book. Dave Williams once again provided his excellent graphic design skills. A true team effort here, once again.

Chuck Wexler
Executive Director, PERF

Foreword

Sixteen years ago, when I was still new to my job as executive director of PERF, I began to attend our annual meetings, where police chiefs from around the nation gather and compare notes about what is happening in their lives.

And what I distinctly remember about those early meetings is that my mouth kept dropping open as I heard one chief after another tell their stories. Stories about battling with police employee unions. About being asked by the mayor or city council members to do things they knew were not right. Uncovering corruption in the ranks. Being sued. Trying to improve the police department and being thwarted by unyielding bureaucracies. Being forced to keep senior managers who sided more with the rank and file than with management. Worrying about a sensational crime that wasn't solved—and all the other crimes that hardly get noticed, except by the victims. And through it all, getting criticized from some angle, no matter what they did.

Over the years, I began to notice that even though new chiefs constantly joined our ranks, the stories they would tell sounded familiar. The details varied, but many of the themes were repeated. And the new chiefs often seemed to think they were the first to deal with these issues.

So it seems that men and women take the job of chief of police, encounter similar types of problems, and struggle with them as if no one had ever experienced them before. Very often, experienced chiefs say in hindsight that when they took their first job as chief, they had little experience to prepare them for what they were about to find.

Bob McNeilly had faced many of these challenges, and he and I decided that it would be terrific if we could capture the experience and lessons learned by a cross-section of police executives. So PERF decided to embark on this project. Our staff interviewed 25 police chiefs about their experiences as chief, asking them dozens of questions about what they have learned over the course of their careers about the job that they do. These chiefs generously gave us their time and insight, in order to help their peers benefit from the lessons they have learned the hard way.

This book breaks down the job of police chief into various chapters—on working with your mayor, your community, and your rank-and-file officers; on developing productive relationships with your local news media; on finding a good fit between your style as a chief and the type of policing that a community is looking for.

But the underlying theme running through this entire project and all of these issues was this: "How can PERF, by tapping into the wisdom of experienced chiefs, help other chiefs avoid rookie mistakes, recognize good opportunities, and become more effective chiefs?"

I believe that due to the candor and insight of the chiefs quoted here, this book will go a long way to helping chiefs do a better job. And I think that readers will find this book interesting, because our 25 chiefs have seen a lot, and they were quite frank about their experiences.

That's not to say that our 25 chiefs never made a mistake. In fact, this book includes their advice about how to minimize the damage from a mistake. (Hint: They don't advise trying to cover it up.)

Some may wonder how we happened to choose the 25 chiefs in this book. On page 3, we describe the rather formal selection process we developed. Of course, there are hundreds of experienced chiefs who could have participated and made strong contributions to a book like this. Our main consideration was that we aimed to have a group with a broad range of backgrounds and experiences.

In other words, the chiefs who are quoted in this book were not chosen because they are paragons of any particular virtue. Rather, they were chosen because they are accomplished, they have experience in different-size agencies across the country (some in one police department, others in several different agencies), and they have a wealth of experience to share—some of it positive, and many negative experiences as well. And they have all been involved with helping PERF in various ways over the years.

Finally, the chiefs in this book have another thing in common. They all have a profound regard for their profession. And each one, in his or her own way, has lessons to share.

I hope that this book will be useful to aspiring chiefs, new chiefs, and experienced chiefs and will serve as a valuable resource in these challenging times.

Chuck Wexler

Chuck Wexler
Executive Director, PERF

Introduction

"On Being A Chief," in Their Own Words

Exploring the Nuances of Being a Police Chief

This book chronicles what a group of experienced police chiefs have to say about the nature of their jobs. It is intended to help men and women who think they might want to be a chief some day, or who are transitioning into the chief's position. This book also is intended for veteran chiefs who could benefit from the experience of their colleagues. The chiefs quoted in this book offer advice about how chiefs can shape their administration, manage their personnel, handle the high-risk decisions that must be made, and keep themselves healthy and whole when the odds seem to be against them. It reflects the Police Executive Research Forum's (PERF) continuing commitment to helping police leaders acquire the knowledge and skills they need to be effective in their jobs and make a difference in the communities they serve.

This book may be seen as a follow-up to PERF's 1986 book, *Managing for Success: A Police Chief's Survival Guide,* and to the 1999 PERF book *Command Performance: Career Guide for Police Executives*. But while *Command Performance* is largely about how to get a job as a police chief, *Leadership Matters* is mainly about how to be an effective and successful chief, and how to avoid the types of mistakes that experienced chiefs say are most common to the job.

This book offers aspiring chiefs guidance in assessing their readiness for the top job and evaluating opportunities to serve as chief. For sitting chiefs and those transitioning from one chief's job to another, this book provides an opportunity to compare

> EVERY CHIEF'S JOB IS A LEARNING EXPERIENCE,
> BUT THE FIRST CHIEF'S JOB IS WHERE YOU
> MAKE ALL THE MISTAKES.
> **–FORMER MINNEAPOLIS CHIEF BOB OLSON**

their thinking to that of other chiefs who have been tested over the course of their careers.

While much of being a chief is about leadership, this book is not simply a leadership guide. Nor does it delve into the strategies that veteran chiefs have employed to address the crime-related problems that a chief will encounter in his or her career.

Instead, this book provides a chief's-eye view of the subtleties of being police chief. "Police chiefs need help in understanding the many nuances of being effective in the job," said retired Chief Darrel Stephens of the Charlotte-Mecklenburg, N.C. Police Department. "All new chiefs bring with them a certain level of experience and knowledge that they will need to be effective. What they may not have is the understanding of how their world changes when they get the top job."

New chiefs in particular, veteran chiefs say, need help in preparing for the magnitude of those changes. "Every chief's job is a learning experience, but the first chief's job is where you make all the mistakes," said former Minneapolis Chief Bob Olson.

Philadelphia Police Commissioner Charles Ramsey added: "Without an appreciation for and understanding of the challenge of acclimating to these changes, new chiefs are forced to find their own way. Some of them get lost, destroying themselves in the first few weeks in office."

A Notable Gap in Guidance

This book aims to fill a sizable gap. Chiefs and policing researchers agree that there are few documents available that offer specific advice on the role of the police chief, aimed at helping an aspiring chief prepare for the job. While chiefs say they often tap into publications on managerial leadership and organization for business and industry, "there is no guide on how to do *this* job," said retired Commissioner Ronnie Watson of the Cambridge, Mass. Police Department.

Policing researchers say that managing a police department is a topic that has not been studied thoroughly. "[It's] second only to [police] unions as an under-investigated area," said Professor Samuel Walker of the University of Nebraska at Omaha, speaking to a group of policing researchers and police chiefs. Even determining the parameters of the topic is difficult. Lois Felson Mock, a social science analyst who is well-respected by police executives for her distinguished work at the National Institute of Justice, attributed the "spottiness" of research on police leadership to the challenge of deciding what to study. "I think it is very difficult to define what the topic area is," Ms. Mock said. "Leadership can mean so many different things, and ranges from decision-making abilities to the organizational and political abilities of big-city chiefs. No wonder we have had a hard time with it."

The PERF Project:
Mining a Wealth of Knowledge and Experience

So, given this acknowledged information gap, where do chiefs turn for the guidance that they need?

Beginning in 2006, PERF began talking to chiefs across the country about how to frame a project that would produce the information that chiefs say they need. Time and again, when asked where they seek advice, chiefs responded that they turn to their colleagues, because veteran chiefs can speak most authoritatively on what the job requires of those who hold it. "Police chiefs don't have a career path," said Milwaukee Police Chief Ed Flynn. He quoted Patrick V. Murphy, the former commissioner of the New York City and Washington, D.C. police departments, who said, "You learn how to be a chief by being a chief."

Taking those comments to heart, PERF researchers embarked on an initiative to tap into this wealth of knowledge through a series of interviews with, and written commentaries from, a cadre of veteran police chiefs. PERF convened a session during its annual meeting to discuss the project and solicit chiefs' advice on topics to be addressed. Following that meeting, PERF convened a Project Resource Group of six veteran chiefs. Project researchers worked with that small group to develop a set of criteria for selecting chiefs to be interviewed. The Resource Group members then were asked to nominate sitting and former chiefs fitting the criteria, and a list of chiefs to be interviewed was developed.

In consultation with Resource Group members, PERF project researchers began setting down on paper the areas of inquiry that would apply to all chiefs during the interviews. Interviewers also devised additional questions for specific chiefs known to have special experience or expertise on particular topics.

The chiefs were chosen for their ability to provide a broad spectrum of advice based on their experiences in small, medium, and large departments with various kinds of political structures and crime problems.

In the end, 25 chiefs were interviewed—23 in person or by telephone, and two who submitted written responses to questions.

These chiefs have a great deal of experience in municipal policing. Nearly all of them have at least 25 years of experience in law enforcement, and half began their policing careers more than 35 years ago. Half of them have spent more than 40 percent of their careers in the top job, as chiefs. About half have served as chief in two or more municipal police departments, and about one-third have served as chief in three or more departments. And they are a well-educated group; most hold master's degrees, and several have law degrees.

The following pages provide the wisdom, on matters large and small, that was generously offered by the 25 experienced chiefs.

NOTE: The chiefs who are quoted in this book are identified by their affiliations at the time they were interviewed. A number of them have recently moved on to head new agencies or have retired.

Chapter 1

A Sense of Passion: How Chiefs View Their Jobs

In this chapter, chiefs share their perspectives on how they view their jobs, and on the qualities and skills they believe they have brought to the job. They talk about what drew them to the job, about their management and leadership styles, about how they measure their own successes, and about the things that wear them down—or cheer them up when times are tough.

How They See the Job

Many described the job of police chief as that of a visionary and strategist. Chiefs are expected to conceptualize a vision for the department; to implement a mission to achieve that vision; and to "sell" that mission both within and outside the department.

Chiefs interviewed for this book said that being a chief is about managing change. "In this profession, change is a constant—and a necessity. From a practical standpoint, it can't be resisted," said Los Angeles Chief Bill Bratton. The relentlessness of the process of change generally yields improvements in policing, he added, citing the emergence of community policing as an example.

Seattle Chief Gil Kerlikowske agreed. "Every chief is hired as a change agent," he said. "The test for a chief is to understand the kind of changes to make, how much change is needed, and how much the department and the elected officials can tolerate."

A critical aspect of the chief's job as change agent is working as a "small-p politician" in order to leverage support for his or her

> EVERY CHIEF IS HIRED AS A CHANGE AGENT. THE TEST FOR A
> CHIEF IS TO UNDERSTAND THE KIND OF CHANGES TO MAKE,
> HOW MUCH CHANGE IS NEEDED, AND HOW MUCH THE
> DEPARTMENT AND THE ELECTED OFFICIALS CAN TOLERATE.
> **—CHIEF GIL KERLIKOWSKE**

vision, chiefs said. The vision itself is likely to be popular; after all, who would object to visionary goals, such as making a city safer and providing a responsive, committed police department? But the decisions that a chief makes in order to *achieve* a vision can be controversial, and doing the right thing, chiefs said, requires making difficult decisions that may be unpopular with politicians, with the rank and file, or with the public. The chief's job as change agent, the chiefs say, is all about making correct decisions and then standing by them.

The Importance of Leading Your Officers

In the end, chiefs said, whether the improvements that a chief makes to a department are maintained over the long run depends on how the chief goes about leading the men and women who take the chief's vision and mission to the street. And leading the department includes defending officers against unfair or excessive criticism.

"Championing our officers should be among our top priorities," one chief said. "It's something most of us don't do a good enough job of. Unlike other jobs, every time a police officer makes a mistake, it winds up in the newspaper." This is a message that this chief says he has taken to his boss, who had openly criticized officers in the news media. "I told the mayor, 'If you criticize officers, that doesn't get to your objective,'" the chief said. Since then, the mayor has been slower to criticize the police.

What Drew Chiefs to the Job

The chiefs were unequivocal about their passion for policing. And most said that the passion took hold of them early in their careers, spurred them up through the ranks through more challenging positions, and ultimately took them to the position of chief.

Chiefs interviewed came to their policing careers by different routes. For some chiefs, it was a natural extension of their military service. Several chiefs chose policing careers after participating in police cadet programs. Another dated his interest in policing to his experience in a police internship that he undertook to comply with his high school's community service requirement.

Asked about their rise to the top job, most chiefs said that attaining some type of leadership role was an ambition from early in their policing careers. However, they said that being *chief* was a goal that evolved as they moved up though the ranks, not an early career aspiration.

For Commissioner Ramsey, a defining moment came when, as a patrolman, he watched a 60-year-old peer struggle physically as he worked his assignment at a crime scene. "I said to myself, 'That can't be me when I'm in my 60s,'" Ramsey said. "So I started studying for the sergeants' exam. Later I reached the rank of lieutenant. That's when I started thinking about working toward becoming chief some day. That's when I realized I had fallen in love with policing."

Chief Stephens said he decided to pursue a chief's job after completing a fellowship with the National Institute of Justice. "My goal was to be chief in a large department, because I thought policing needed to change, and that was one of the best positions to make the change," he explained.

Chief Kerlikowske credited his interest in becoming a chief to exposure to good role models as he rose up through the ranks. These role models, he said, were progressive in their thinking about policing. They talked about "education, innovation, being more of a partner with the community, and team policing"—all of which became part of Kerlikowske's own value system.

San Diego Chief William Lansdowne said that when he began his career in policing, he was not thinking of becoming chief one day. "My goal was to get to be lieutenant," he said. "And then when I made lieutenant, I realized that you can become chief if you work hard at it and have some kind of plan."

THE UNMARKED ROAD TO BECOMING A POLICE CHIEF: A JOURNEY WORTH TAKING

By PERF President John F. Timoney
Chief of Police, Miami, Florida

It's becoming more difficult to find people willing to apply for the position of chief of police.

I have some perspective on this, because my first experience applying for a chief's job was 18 years ago. I was a young guy and I wanted to see what the process was like. So as a bit of a lark, I applied to be the police chief in Phoenix.

I think they started with 56 candidates, and I survived the winnowing-down to the final six. They brought the six of us in for interviews, and it was a very impressive process. There were three days of interviews. First we were questioned by a group of business leaders, including the head of the top TV station and some bankers. The next day it was community groups, and the third day was the city council and the city manager.

Even though I didn't get the job, I left Phoenix with a very good feeling about the whole process and how professionally it was handled. There was a feeling of legitimacy about it; you were treated like a professional.

Now it's different in a lot of ways, and I don't mean better.

There seems to be a feeling that if you work in policing, it's somehow disloyal to apply for a bigger job. If you're already a chief and you are seen to apply at another agency, your officers—and your mayor—say, "Look, he's trying to get out of here." If you don't succeed in getting the new job, the fact that you looked elsewhere is going to make things difficult for you in your current job.

This dampens the ambition of assistant or deputy chiefs. If you're a deputy in City A and you apply to become the chief in City B or C, you'd better hope you get the job, because you may have damaged your chances if the chief position in City A opens up.

Second, job searches have become quite uncomfortable. It's almost like a blood sport now; you really are thrown into the arena. You think you're a pretty decent person, and you innocently put in to be police chief somewhere, and suddenly there are all sorts of people with political agendas surfacing to attack you. You don't even know these people, you're not even from the same city. But they're saying you're "too much this" or "not enough that," and they're tearing you apart. And you think, "Where is all this anger coming from? All I did was interview for a job."

And it's not just the political groups, it's the police unions. About 10 years ago, police unions began to organize toward removing chiefs. At police unions' national conventions they actually have sessions where they train their membership in "how to take out a chief" with votes of no-confidence and other tactics. If you're an assistant chief and you watch the battles between the chief of police and the unions, you start to think, "I've got a nice position, a decent salary—why would I want the top job?" If you do take the plunge and apply for a chief's job, you'll find that the unions will check out all the candidates. If you haven't gotten along with the unions in your hometown, you'll be excoriated as being hostile to unions and unable to get along with other people.

So if you're a young assistant chief ready to take the plunge, it can be a bit unsteadying. All of these things come together, and you start to worry that this is a lot more difficult than it should be.

Running a police organization is much more complex than it was a generation ago, and more than ever, we need good, talented people with a broad world view to step forward. While there is no prescribed roadmap to becoming a chief other than actual executive experience, the single most promising executive development program for aspiring police leaders is PERF's Senior Management Institute for Police. As chief in Miami, I have sent virtually my entire command staff to this outstanding program.

This book is another effort by PERF to help cultivate the next generation of police leaders. In these pages, you'll find 25 experienced police chiefs talking about their jobs, with an eye toward guiding up-and-coming police leaders who think they might want to be a chief some day.

We need to reassure our younger colleagues that even though this process of becoming a chief looks tough, you can get through it.

And we should constantly tell them that while it's great being a Number 2 or Number 3 person in an organization, where there's not too much pressure, there is *nothing* like the reward and satisfaction of actually running a police agency.

[ON ADVANCING ONE'S CAREER IN A POLICE DEPARTMENT]
IF THERE'S A PROBLEM, YOU WANT TO BE THE PERSON
THAT THE CHIEF COMES TO IN ORDER TO FIX IT. THE PEOPLE
WHO GET PROMOTED ARE THE ONES WHO ARE WILLING
TO PUT THE TIME IN, WHO DON'T COMPLAIN, AND
WHO MAKE THINGS HAPPEN.
—CHIEF WILLIAM LANSDOWNE

What kind of plan? "You need to look at the people who are successful and see how they did that," Lansdowne said. "And part of the secret, I've always thought, is staying out of the inter-office politics. Many people kind of attach themselves to a commander, hoping they'll be dragged along if that person rises. But I think you're much better off focusing on being good at what you do, being successful, and making yourself the go-to person. If there's a problem, you want to be the person that the chief comes to in order to fix it. The people who get promoted are the ones who are willing to put the time in, who don't complain, and who make things happen."

Their Leadership Styles

Asked to describe their "style" of running a police department, most chiefs said they are consensus builders and they follow a democratic approach to leading their departments. "What I try to do is present a problem or issue, get feedback from everyone, try to develop consensus, and rely on the direction that I receive from the mayor, the community, and from within the department to drive toward the mayor's and the community's goals," said Boston Police Commissioner Ed Davis.

"I'm not a dictator; I'm a consensus builder," said retired Milwaukee Chief Nan Hegerty. Chief Hegerty said she made a point of spending time in the field talking to officers, a practice that she believes produced more candid insights from the officers, who felt more comfortable speaking out when their direct supervisors were not around.

Lenexa, Kan. Chief Ellen Hanson described herself as a "big picture" manager who does not micro-manage, but rather gives her officers a great deal of autonomy to make decisions in the field about what actions will serve the community best. And, she said, she lets them know that she will be firmly in their corner if they have exercised good judgment and acted reasonably. "I tell them, 'If you are doing the right thing for the right reason, I'll stand behind you,'" she said.

Chief David Kunkle of Dallas described his management style as one of prodding his employees to think, question, consider new concepts, and take the risk of sharing their opinions and ideas.

Some chiefs interviewed for this book described themselves as "trouble-shooters"—chiefs who have an affinity for taking on leadership responsibilities in troubled departments. "No one hires me as a maintenance person," said Savannah, Ga. Chief Michael Berkow.

Chief Bratton is another chief who sees himself as a risk-taker who "purposefully seeks out organizations that are in crisis," and who aims to bring experience and leadership to departments in order to fix problems.

Chief Lansdowne said that one thing that has worked for him is a "hands-on" style of managing his employees. "You've got to be approachable, available, and you've got to be seen in the organization," he said. "It's a simple thing to walk into the Records Department and say hello, to Communications, to the Information Technologies unit, and check on everybody. It makes people feel very valuable. I want to know people by name. When I got here [as chief in San Diego], they had a yearbook with the names and pictures of everybody in the department, and I'd study the book and see who was who in the department. Some of them were floored because they'd never met me, but I knew what their names were. That relationship-building is important. You've got to make people understand that they're important, whatever their job is, and to understand how they fit into the entire process."

What Brings Them Down . . . What Lifts Them Up

Chiefs said the injury or death of a police officer, or of a citizen at the hands of a police officer, is the most difficult situation that a chief may face. And chiefs said their greatest disappointments come when a police officer is found to have engaged in misconduct. The disappointment is compounded when other officers do not come forward and report malfeasance, despite the chief's best efforts to instill a greater sense of individual responsibility among officers, Stephens said. It is also discouraging when employees

> THE RESPONSIBILITIES OF RUNNING AN ORGANIZATION
> THAT OPERATES 24/7, WHERE THINGS CAN GO TOTALLY
> HAYWIRE BASED ON THE ACTIONS OF ONE OR TWO
> OFFICERS—EVEN WHEN THE OFFICERS OPERATE
> WITH THE BEST JUDGMENT AND INTENTIONS—
> CAN BE OVERWHELMING.
> **—CHIEF DARREL STEPHENS**

who show a great deal of promise do not live up to that potential, he said, because a chief sees that failure as his own failure to help them achieve more.

Equally discouraging, Stephens said, is the constant need to deal with the political side of running a police department. "You soon come to understand that no decision can be made that will be universally accepted," he said.

Finally, Stephens said, for a police chief, there is no one to blame but yourself when something goes wrong. "The responsibilities of running an organization that operates 24/7, where things can go totally haywire based on the actions of one or two officers—even when the officers operate with the best judgment and intentions—can be overwhelming," he said. "In other jobs, you can pass the responsibility on to someone else. But people look to a police chief to be responsible for things that are perceived to be within the control of the police."

Chiefs say their love of their job buoys them up when times are tough. After Chief Bob McNeilly moved on from the Pittsburgh Bureau of Police after leading it for nearly a decade, "A lot of people said, 'I guess you're glad to be away,'" he said. "I told them no, I enjoyed every day. Maybe being a risk-taker is about the excitement. You have the joys when you're successful and feel that you have had some impact."

Chief Charlie Deane of Prince William County, Va. joined the Police Department there in 1970 and was named chief in 1988, but said he has not burned out in the job. Why not? "Because it's still fun," he said. "I still enjoy having a role in working with the community and helping dedicated police officers succeed in their careers." And for Deane, one of the most interesting parts is having overall responsibility for major criminal investigations. "It's still a thrill to be involved in learning the details of a case, in making sure we're bringing all the pieces of a case together," he said. "I try to stay back far enough so I don't interfere, but I'm still interested in the details of investigations, and for me that's very rewarding."

Pasadena, Calif. Chief Bernard Melekian, like a number of other chiefs, said he gains strength during the difficult times from his essential respect for his job and the people who work for him.

"This may come across as a little corny, but I really believe that first and foremost, you have to love cops and you have to love police work," Melekian said. "In fact, I'm a little concerned that too often we tell our young captains that being a police chief is a horrible job, that it's stressful and it'll ruin your marriage and ruin your life," Melekian added. "I suppose it can if you let it. But I'm here to tell you that even on a bad day, being a police chief is a wonderfully rewarding position."

The rewards, Retired Superintendent Phil Cline of Chicago said, often come in small ways. Cline said he was heartened by chance encounters with young officers whose deference and respect for him underscored the importance of the position of authority that had been entrusted to him. He said that it is important to make the time to recognize and acknowledge the hard work of your officers. One of his favorite duties was presiding at monthly awards ceremonies, where he never tired of being approached by an officer asking to have his or her picture taken with the superintendent. Despite the grueling schedule of leading the department, "When I got to spend 10 minutes with a group of young cops, that recharged me for the day," he said.

Chief Melekian agreed about recognizing the hard work of front-line officers. "I often tell my command staff, only half-jokingly, that we don't do any real work anymore," he said. "The real work is done by the young men and women who drive the radio cars, who answer the phone, who talk to the public. Our job is to make their job possible. I'm not diminishing the chief's role, but it's important to remember that it's not about you, it's about the officers who do the real work."

Chief Dean Esserman of Providence said that he is sustained by the knowledge that his officers can perform well without his constant attention. When he needed to take leave to recover from an illness, he said, "People wondered, 'How will the team stay together while the team captain is away?' But they all saw that the team *did* stay together—and that's not how it was in the past. That was very satisfying to me."

Sometimes police chiefs get an "ah-ha moment"—a sudden victory that can make the sting of defeats fade, Bratton said. For example, he cited a time when he was able to find a loophole in hiring regulations that allowed him to create civilian positions and bring "outsiders" onto his command staff. (The extent to which chiefs are allowed to choose their own command leadership is discussed further in Chapter 4, "Developing and Empowering Your Command Team.")

How They Stay Focused, Centered, and Fit

The trick to keeping focused and fit on the job, chiefs said, is to learn to "compartmentalize"—to find a way to separate the job from other aspects of your life. This is not easy, chiefs admit. Being chief is an around-the-clock job, and most chiefs said they have little time away from the job and even fewer occasions where the job is not on their mind, even if at a subconscious level.

"I don't relax all that much. My way of relaxing is to get out in a scout car," said Ramsey. "But I have learned to compartmentalize." Many chiefs suffer from not knowing how to temporarily put away thoughts about problems in the police department, Ramsey said. "You've got to have 'parking lots' in your mind for some of this," he said.

Chief Hegerty spoke of compartmentalization in a different way. "I approach my job as just one facet of my life. There's my professional life, my personal life, and my spiritual life. And I think all three of those have to be equal. The job of a police chief is always on your mind. Every time the phone rings, a chief will worry that it may be another crisis. But there will come a time when you're going to leave the job, and if you don't have a strong relationship with your spouse and something to go to, you're going to be lost. I just think you need to keep your life balanced."

Chief Flynn said he has learned to maintain a level of emotional and intellectual detachment that helps him avoid personalizing what he experiences in his professional life—in other words, "building a bit more space between me and the job." Flynn also said that "breaks" in his policing career, times when he worked in city business administration and for a state public safety agency, helped him "get reenergized and recharged" for going back into police agency administration.

Chief Melekian said that for him, time spent reading for pleasure reduces stress, because depending on what he's reading

[ON WAYS TO RELIEVE STRESS]
I DRINK A BUD LIGHT AND SMOKE A CIGAR. OR I GO FOR A
DRIVE IN MY CORVETTE. AND SUNDAY MORNINGS, I GET UP
AT 5:30, GO OUTSIDE, AND WATCH THE SUN COME UP, AND
LIFE IS GOOD. THERE'S A LOT TO BE THANKFUL FOR.
—CHIEF WILLIAM LANSDOWNE

about, "it often reminds me that whatever stresses I'm facing, people have faced things 10, 20, 100 times worse."

"And I've learned that no matter how bad something might feel at night, if you can just go to sleep, you get up the next day and it'll be better," Melekian added. "It always is."

Chief Kunkle keeps fit by running marathons. He added that the job of police chief itself can be a reenergizing force because of the constant changes occurring in a police department. Even when he served for 14 years as chief in Arlington, Texas before taking the top job in Dallas, there were constantly new faces in the department, he said. "I went through three and a half command staffs in that department, and so I was lucky that there were always new good people."

Flynn said he has found that surprisingly, "the more difficult the challenges, the less stress I feel. The stress seldom comes from the difficulty of the mission. It's the personnel issues and politics that can wear you down."

Another chief chuckled when asked what he does to manage the stress of his job, because he finds it invigorating rather than tiring. "Some people say I need to recharge my batteries," Miami Chief John Timoney said. "But I don't. I work out every day. I never feel tired by the job."

Lansdowne said he has several ways of relieving stress. "I drink a Bud Light and smoke a cigar. Or I go for a drive in my Corvette. And Sunday mornings, I get up at 5:30, go outside, and watch the sun come up, and life is good. There's a lot to be thankful for."

How Chiefs Gauge Whether They're Doing a Good Job

Never be complacent in your job, chiefs advised. Chiefs should never believe they have achieved their optimal level of performance.

"The worst thing you can do is feel that you have hit your stride," Ramsey said. "You have to greet each day as a new challenge. You never have it licked. You will get lax if you think that you do."

Instead, Ramsey said, chiefs can hope to arrive at a point where they feel comfortable in their jobs. "You learn through experience, and you can get to a comfort level," he said. Ramsey said he found his comfort level during his tenure at the Washington, D.C. Metropolitan Police Department, during the department's successful handling of a major national protest in the city. The department drew high praise from community leaders and protestors alike for its handling of that event, and "the pride came back" to the agency, Ramsey said. He began to feel truly comfortable leading the department.

Ramsey also advised his colleagues to write a note to themselves about what they hope to achieve, put it in an envelope, and tuck that note away in a drawer, to be taken out and reviewed every time they have a wildly successful or a depressingly difficult day. They should reflect on what they wrote down in that note and develop a new resolve to wake up the next morning and keep working toward those goals, he said. "Don't get caught up in the drama of the job, or the glitz, or the day-to-day difficulties," Ramsey said. "Keep focused on that little envelope in your desk."

Because police chiefs tend not to have long tenures in the job, "I think we sometimes make an assumption that survival is a benchmark for success," said Milliken, Colo. Chief Jim Burack. "But we should never lose focus that the most important benchmark is the public safety value that the chief helps produce for the community." Other chiefs agreed, saying that when they left a department, they looked back on their tenure and were gratified to see that crime levels had declined, or training of officers had been improved, or police misconduct had been reduced, and so on.

Berkow added that departing chiefs trying to gauge their performance should also watch to see how many of their accomplishments remain in effect after they leave. "It's like bending a steel bar," he said. "You grab, bend, and measure where it goes when you let go."

Retired Commissioner Watson said he expects that he will be remembered for advocating and overseeing the construction of new police buildings for the department in Cambridge, Mass. But in his own view, his greatest accomplishment was the adoption of ethical rules—standards that he believes "will probably last for a long time to come."

Chapter 2

Before You Take the Top Job: Assessing "The Fit"

The ability of a chief to lead a department will depend upon whether he or she is the right person for that particular job, many chiefs emphasized. "It's all about fit," said Colorado Springs Chief Rick Myers.

To determine whether you will be a good fit for a particular department, you first must know yourself, chiefs said. "Whether you 'find a home' in a department depends on the type of personality you have and your core values," said Flynn. Those core values become the foundation of a chief's leadership of a police department, and the benchmarks for its performance. A chief's core values have to match those of the community if the chief is to have a productive relationship with the department.

Do you have the qualities and character of a leader?

But first, aspiring chiefs should assess whether they have what it takes to lead *any* police department. Asked what makes a good chief, chiefs interviewed for this book said that the defining qualification for the job is a love of policing and a passion for *doing* the job. Wanting the job is not enough. "If all you want is to *be* the chief, you're probably not right for the job," Ramsey said. "But if you think that you can take people where they haven't been before and do something positive, you probably are a good candidate for chief."

YOU HAVE TO REALLY UNDERSTAND THE JOB. YOU CAN'T
BRING IN SOMEBODY WHO HAS A PH.D. BUT HAS NO IDEA
OF WHAT IT'S LIKE TO HAVE SOMEBODY SPIT IN YOUR
FACE—OR ALMOST KILL YOU WITH A KNIFE OR A GUN.
OFFICERS ARE PUT IN VERY DIFFICULT CIRCUMSTANCES. . .
[I]F YOU'VE BEEN THERE, AND YOU CAN RELATE TO
WHAT THE OFFICER WAS GOING THROUGH, YOU CAN
MAKE BETTER DECISIONS.
—CHIEF CHARLIE DEANE

Chiefs must be open, honest, transparent, sincere, and have a strong work ethic, chiefs said. "Be straightforward, and be who you are. Be accountable, and acknowledge the mistakes that you make," said Chief Bob McNeilly, who now serves in Elizabeth Township, Pa. after a decade as chief in Pittsburgh. "And be honest. You want to be viewed as somebody who is going to say the same thing to two different people," not someone who will change the message to appease each party to a disagreement.

Melekian agreed that a strong sense of honesty is critical to a chief's success. "I think people will put up with a leader that they may not agree with, if they feel that the processes around that person are fair and transparent and consistent," he said. "If you're delivering bad news or you've got to make a tough decision, there's nothing wrong with telling people why you're making it, even if they don't like it. If you're not able to do that, and people start to think that you're not communicating forthrightly with them, you begin to lose the engagement of those people you need to work with."

Chiefs should have an ability to show restraint in the use of the authority that comes with the job. The measure of the character of a police chief, Chief Olson said, is the ability to "exercise restraint in the use of the awesome power we have." Olson recounted his experience with an officer who wanted to rise in rank because he saw it as a way to "get the power." But in the end, he said, the ability and character of chiefs should be measured "by how much they *didn't* use that power."

Lansdowne said that a talent for listening to people is critical to being a police chief. "You've got to learn to listen, and to invite criticism," he said. "If you don't do that, and your employees are

> SOMEBODY ASKED WAYNE GRETZKY, "WHY ARE YOU SUCH A
> GREAT HOCKEY PLAYER?" GRETZKY SAID, "BECAUSE I SKATE
> TO WHERE THE PUCK IS GOING TO BE." I THINK IT'S THE
> CHIEF'S JOB TO ALWAYS WATCH THE PUCK AND FIGURE OUT
> WHERE IT'S GOING TO BE, AND TO PLAN ACCORDINGLY.
> **—CHIEF BERNARD MELEKIAN**

afraid to tell you what's going on, you'll get in trouble quickly. You need to have a relationship with them and an open policy that says, 'Look, if there's an issue, tell me, and I'll reward you for it and thank you for letting me know.' And those are the people I promote."

Chief Deane said that several qualities came to his mind as being essential for a police chief—beginning with a clear sense of right and wrong. "Honesty and integrity are the first things you need, because as chief you're thrown into all kinds of situations and pressures, so you need to have a good compass," he said. "And second, I think a chief has to have some self-confidence. You need to be decisive. The worst thing you can have is a chief who can't make up his mind." Third, Deane said, "you have to really understand the job. You can't bring in somebody who has a Ph.D. but has no idea of what it's like to have somebody spit in your face—or almost kill you with a knife or a gun. Officers are put in very difficult circumstances, and sometimes they're not going to react perfectly, and when an officer's action is put under a microscope after the fact, it may look worse than it really is. But if you've been there, and you can relate to what the officer was going through, you can make better decisions. So I think that having experience on the front lines is a requirement." Finally, Deane said, "you have to be good with people. You have to really care about people as individuals. That doesn't mean you have to be out there glad-handing all the time, but you need to be able to communicate well with people."

Melekian said he believes a chief needs to bring a sense of vision and a sense of strategy to the job. "Somebody asked Wayne Gretzky, 'Why are you such a great hockey player?'" Melekian recalled. "Gretzky said, 'Because I skate to where the puck is *going to* be.' I think it's the chief's job to always watch the puck and figure out where it's going to be, and to plan accordingly," Melekian said.

For example, Melekian said that when he took the chief's job in Pasadena, homicides were averaging 25 per year—in a city with only 130,000 residents. "And all these horrific crimes were just sort of accepted as business as usual," he said. For Melekian, seeing the puck where it was going to be meant envisioning a city where high levels of violence would no longer be tolerated. "There were people who told me not to say that, because they thought we couldn't fix the problem," he said. But he launched a gang violence reduction program called "No More Dead Children," which did prove very successful in reducing homicides to about three or four annually in most recent years. The key, Melekian said, was to truly focus on the problem. "Every new idea, every new proposal was run though the filter of 'Does this advance the cause of No More Dead Children?'" he said. "And if it didn't advance that mission, for the most part we didn't approve it."

Do you possess the necessary skills to do the job?

Experienced chiefs said they believe that "essential skill set" for the job includes good oral and written communication skills, strong analytical skills, and the ability to assess a situation objectively. Chiefs must be open to other perspectives and willing to take these perspectives into consideration in making decisions, they added.

Chiefs also must be able to deal constructively with criticism, and willing to listen to their critics and try to help critics understand the choice that the chief has made. They must avoid making commitments that they may not be able to keep, but they also must be decisive.

Chiefs also must avoid being too rigid in dealing with subordinates, in the view of Houston Chief Harold Hurtt. "If you're too heavy-handed, you create a work environment where officers just try to avoid conflict," he said, "so they end up operating on the premise that 'If we don't do anything, we won't get in trouble.'"

Melekian said chiefs must be able to relate to people outside the quasi-military environment of a police department. "Once I heard someone say that police chiefs fail because it's the first time they ever worked for a civilian," he said. "I think there's a ring of truth to that, because most of us came up through a system with people who, whether we liked them or not, thought just like us.

And now, all of a sudden, you're exposed to a mayor or a city manager or a council, and they think very differently from you. I think a lot of chiefs have a problem because they want to stick with the autocratic, hierarchical structure that they're used to, but they've landed in a different arena."

Chiefs also need a great deal of patience, Melekian said. "It is very demanding to be a police chief. And the worst of it isn't the crises—dealing with crime, managing civil disturbances or natural disasters. From my perspective, those are the easy things. The hard things involve listening to people, even when you're tired and it's the end of the day and you've already heard it a half-dozen times. You have to listen to your people, you have to listen to the community, you have to listen to City Hall."

Can you handle the risk associated with being a change agent?

If you have a passion for policing and believe you have the qualities, character, and skills of a leader, then you should consider whether you are sufficiently motivated and have "the right stuff" to take on the riskiness of the job, chiefs said.

Flynn suggested that there are two types of chiefs: risk-takers and "maintenance managers." The risk-takers are change agents and troubleshooters. By contrast, a maintenance manager has a conservative personality and values stability and predictability, he said. Maintenance-manager chiefs "become rooted in the community and find a role they can fill forever," Flynn said, "while change-agents tend towards imposing term limits on themselves."

Other chiefs interviewed for this book said that being a change agent and risk-taker is the hallmark of any chief's job. "Here's the

> HERE'S THE THING: IF THINGS WERE GOING SWELL, THEY WOULDN'T HAVE BROUGHT YOU IN ANYWAY, WOULD THEY? IF THEY BROUGHT YOU IN, IT'S BECAUSE SOMETHING IS WRONG. PEOPLE ARE EXPECTING CHANGE IN PERSONNEL AND POLICIES, SO DON'T DISAPPOINT THEM.
> —CHIEF JOHN TIMONEY

thing: If things were going swell, they wouldn't have brought you in anyway, would they?" said Chief Timoney. "If they brought you in, it's because something is wrong. People are expecting change in personnel and policies, so don't disappoint them."

Other chiefs agreed. "If you are someone who is not willing to take that risk, policing probably is not a good career to jump into. You know the chief's job is not going to last forever," said McNeilly. "You have to be up for that kind of challenge."

Olson was even blunter: "You need to know the boundaries of reasonable risk, but if survival is an issue, you shouldn't be chief. If you can't take risks, get out of the business."

"There are casualties associated with taking risks," said Colonel Esserman. "You have to accept that sooner or later you will be a casualty. Leadership is lonely, and sometimes the only warm blanket you have at night is your beliefs."

Do you have the toughness and confidence to do the right thing?

Managing the risk associated with being a chief demands toughness, confidence, and the ability to look at difficult situations as challenges—for example, "being able to make decisions where there are no really good options," said Stephens.

"You have to be psychologically tough," Ramsey said. "When you're confronted with a big problem, you have to have a sense that you will be able to figure it out. Maybe you didn't create the problem, but you have to fix it. While you have the job, the responsibility is yours. And don't carry the guilt. Sort it out and look at it in a way that doesn't create more stress for you."

[ON THE INHERENT HAZARDS OF
BRINGING CHANGE TO AN ORGANIZATION]
YOU NEED TO KNOW THE BOUNDARIES OF REASONABLE RISK,
BUT IF SURVIVAL IS AN ISSUE, YOU SHOULDN'T BE CHIEF.
IF YOU CAN'T TAKE RISKS, GET OUT OF THE BUSINESS.
—CHIEF ROBERT OLSON

On The Issue of Ego

All of the chiefs said that having an intact ego is a critical element of being tough and confident enough to do the job of being a police chief. But they cautioned against excessive self-promotion. "Chiefs need to have a healthy ego, but keep it in check," said Stephens.

"I prefer the 'servant leader' approach to being a chief over the 'ego visibility' model," said Chief Myers. "Introspection is a quality that I greatly admire in leaders, and that means the ability to look in the mirror, rather than point out the window, when things go wrong. I believe that the strong but low-profile, 'non–charismatic' chiefs are the ones who succeed. I get a little distressed about how much ego I see among law enforcement leaders today—even in five-member departments. When you are drawing the spotlight on yourself, you are not shining it on what's good about your organization," Myers said.

"Egomaniacs do not generally make good chiefs," Hegerty said.

Leadership Style as an Element of "Fit"

Sometimes, a chief's management style must be considered as an element of whether a certain department will be a good "fit," chiefs indicated. Or a chief may need to adjust his or her management style in order to make a good fit in a particular situation.

A new chief needs to adopt a style of leadership that depends on the situation at hand, Berkow said. "You need to assess the competence of your people," he said. "Do they know what they are doing? Do they practice contemporary policing? And you need to look at whether they have a commitment to the chief's vision, to the community's goals. In one department, I needed to make some drastic changes very quickly, because the department was in the midst of a scandal and a crisis. But I was given no authority to change the command staff. So I had to adopt a fairly autocratic style. When I left, I was satisfied that I had done everything I could do, and the

> YOU KNOW THE CHIEF'S JOB IS NOT GOING TO LAST FOREVER. YOU HAVE TO BE UP FOR THAT KIND OF CHALLENGE.
> —CHIEF ROBERT MCNEILLY

community was much happier with the Police Department. Crime was down; we were more connected to the community; we had state-of-the-art dispatch and technology, great training, a lot of less-lethal equipment, new facilities, including a firing range, lots of grant money; etc. But I was very concerned about whether the changes would be sustained. I had made changes not with the support of the command staff, but rather in spite of them."

In general, though, chiefs must be willing to empower command personnel to do their jobs, Olson said. "If you don't want to give up power, you shouldn't be chief," he said. "I met regularly with my people so everyone would know what's going on. I let them know that these meetings were not just for them. 'These meetings are for me,' I would tell them. 'Tell me what's going on.' And I gave them the chance to show what they could do. They knew where I wanted to go, but they designed the nuts and bolts. Because you have a lot of experience, you've seen all of the mistakes, so there's a temptation to intervene too much. But bite your tongue and let them go at it. Let them make mistakes and don't punish them for it."

"I empowered these folks," Olson said. "And when I evaluated them, I looked to see if they were empowering their people. A chief's focus should always be to make folks as good as they can be, and then recognize them for their accomplishments."

Kunkle said that not everyone functions well under his management style of challenging officers and prodding them to think, question, and come up with new ideas. "I've been around long enough to know that just because a command staff member is good at taking directions, it doesn't necessarily follow that they'll be good at taking risks," he said. "There are lots of people who can't make that transition. There's a police culture that rewards conformity and obedience and tends to punish people who take risks. At every place I have been, there are people who are comfortable

> THERE'S A POLICE CULTURE THAT REWARDS CONFORMITY AND OBEDIENCE AND TENDS TO PUNISH PEOPLE WHO TAKE RISKS. AT EVERY PLACE I HAVE BEEN, THERE ARE PEOPLE WHO ARE COMFORTABLE WITH THE WAY THINGS ARE. YOU JUST HAVE TO WORK AROUND THEM UNTIL THEY RETIRE.
> —CHIEF DAVID KUNKLE

with the way things are. You just have to work around them until they retire."

Do Your Homework

Years before they reach the point of applying for a chief's position, aspiring chiefs should prepare for the job by:

- Taking advantage of any opportunities that present themselves to develop leadership and administrative skills.
- Observing the leadership styles and practices of colleagues they admire and respect, and tapping these individuals for advice.
- Attending professional development programs.
- Reading a wide variety of materials about policing and the world. As one chief put it, "read everything."

When an opportunity to become chief presents itself:

- Research the history, practices, reputation, and performance of the department that you hope to lead.
- Make certain that the community has the qualities, values, and views on law enforcement that are most important to you.
- Prepare yourself for the rigors of the selection process.

Pursuing Leadership Opportunities

Chief Hurtt said that in today's environment, aspiring chiefs should prepare for the job by trying to get as much exposure as possible to all aspects of managing a police department. "Don't hide in one area all your career, and then say, 'I want to be chief,'" he said. "You can't get too much exposure to labor-management relations, administration, budget forecasting, dealing with the national government, and even with international agencies. And you need to know how to work with the news media."

Deane agreed that having experience in various areas of a police department is invaluable in taking on the top job. Deane spent several years on patrol, then went into criminal investigations, and later set up an internal affairs office in Prince William County. "I think the experience in internal affairs was perhaps the most eye-opening," he said, "because I got to work with all parts of

[ON USING THE HIGH VISIBILITY OF THE
CHIEF'S POSITION TO ACCOMPLISH YOUR GOALS]
A CHIEF'S STATUS, RECOGNIZABILITY, AND VISIBILITY
ARE PART OF HIS OR HER LEADERSHIP. THEY CAN BE
IMPORTANT TOOLS TO WORKING WITH PEOPLE TO
ACHIEVE CHANGE. I TRY TO USE MY VISIBILITY TO LEVERAGE
POLITICAL AND FINANCIAL SUPPORT FOR PROGRAMS
THAT ARE IMPORTANT TO MY AGENCY.
—CHIEF WILLIAM BRATTON

the department and also work with the public. I think that overall experience in the department helped give me credibility as well as a broad view of the department."

One critical area for a chief is budgeting, Deane added. "Fortunately for me, when I became deputy chief, it was pretty clear that I had a good chance of being appointed chief—that's why they selected me for first deputy—so I had the luxury of being deputy for a couple years," he said. "During that time I got into the details of the budget. I had a great staff who spent time with me on that, and that gave me confidence about budgeting when I became chief."

Melekian agreed about the importance of financial experience and a wide range of other experience. "It's very clear to me that knowing how the money moves is one of the most important skills a chief can have," he said. "And any assignment that takes you out of the traditional crime-fighting mode, and helps you realize the broader impact that police can have in the community, is a good thing."

As an example, Melekian said that as a young lieutenant in Santa Monica, Calif., he was ordered to serve as the police department liaison to a task force on homelessness, and initially he thought he would not like the assignment. But as he got involved in dealing with the severe homelessness problem in that city, he found that such assignments "can help you appreciate the role that policing plays in the social fabric, the social network."

Hurtt said aspiring chiefs should also look for knowledge and experience outside the world of policing. "You need to go out and see what the rest of the world is doing," he said.

Early in her policing career, Detroit Chief Ella Bully-Cummings was laid off by her department for four years due to a budget

I DON'T KNOW HOW YOU CAN BE AN EFFECTIVE LEADER
IF YOU DON'T HAVE A FORMAL EDUCATION, BECAUSE
THAT'S WHERE YOU LEARN A LOT OF THE SKILLS THAT ARE
IMPORTANT IN BEING SUCCESSFUL—ORGANIZATIONAL
SKILLS, FINANCIAL SKILLS, STRATEGIC PLANNING . . . .
WE'RE RUNNING VERY COMPLEX AGENCIES TODAY.
—CHIEF ELLA BULLY-CUMMINGS

crisis. During that time, she worked as an assistant to a newspaper executive. She said her experience at the newspaper marked the beginning of her education in management and administration and helped to shape her orientation toward the business end of policing.

Bully-Cummings, who earned a bachelor's degree in public administration while working as a police officer and then obtained a law degree, also said that she advises aspiring chiefs to pursue higher education. "Policing is now a profession," she said. "It isn't as simple as it used to be, where you could just join a police department and put on a gun. What we do today requires a lot more intellectual skill. And for senior leaders in a department, especially in a major city department, I don't know how you can be an effective leader if you don't have a formal education, because that's where you learn a lot of the skills that are important in being successful—organizational skills, financial skills, strategic planning, those kinds of things. We're running very complex agencies today."

Join professional organizations and take advantage of the continuing education programs that these organizations offer, and the opportunity that their membership meetings afford to learn from your colleagues, chiefs said.

Get to Know the Community— and Look for a Good Fit With Your Experience

When an aspiring chief reaches the point of applying for his or her first position as chief, it is important to research the department and the city to ensure that the job will be a good match, chiefs agreed.

Know what qualities you most value in a community. Chief Stephens said that his optimal job is in a community that has "a reputation for good government" and embraces community-oriented and problem-solving policing. To determine whether a community meets these criteria, Stephens said he talks to the incumbent chief and others who are familiar with the department and the community, both inside and outside the department. He also searches the Internet for news accounts about the community and its police force to gain insight into the history of the department, the police culture, the chief's tenure, and the labor climate. A candidate also will want to examine policy and operational changes that need to be made in order to meet the bosses' expectations, he added.

"If it looks like a no-win situation, it probably is," Stephens said. "If I had it to do over, I would skip one city where my tenure as chief turned out to be a bad experience, even though I fully understood what I was getting into and was confident I could succeed." If you go against your instincts and take a job, go in with your eyes open and be prepared to accept the consequences, he advised.

Flynn, who has worked in six different departments of various sizes, five as chief of police, suggested that aspiring officers should think about what kind of department they would like to lead and then try to gain experience in the types of departments that will produce a good fit.

For example, Flynn began his career in Jersey City, N.J., a tough, urban environment directly across the Hudson River from New York City, with the second-largest police force in New Jersey. After working his way up through the ranks to the level of inspector, he took the job of chief in Braintree, Mass. "I had been in a big department with about 1,000 cops, and I knew a lot about police work and a fair amount about supervision and management," he said. "But when I took over that department of 80 officers in bucolic Braintree, I was surprised at the personal toll that it can take. Larger is busier, but because larger tends to be about larger issues, it feels less personal and therefore less painful. The challenge I found in Braintree was that the chief in an environment like that can't escape the personal side of politics, the personal side of labor relations, the personal side of personnel decisions such as discipline or transfers. It's always in his face; it's wired into the community gossip/Little League/school/parish network. There's virtually no escaping it, and that can be debilitating. Chiefs in that position, because their management staffs are smaller, are not even a little bit insulated from the consequences of every single

[ON THE DIFFERENT DYNAMICS OF
MANAGING A SMALL POLICE DEPARTMENT:]
WE'RE REGULARLY ON THE STREET. WE WRITE TRAFFIC
TICKETS, WE GO OUT ON PATROL. AND YOU GET DIRECT
CONTACT WITH PEOPLE AND THEIR COMPLAINTS....
IF YOU'RE A GOOD SMALL-AGENCY CHIEF, YOU'RE IN
TUNE WITH WHAT'S HAPPENING AT THE RETAIL LEVEL.
SO IT'S MUCH LESS LIKELY THAT YOU'LL GET BLINDSIDED
BY ANYTHING, BECAUSE YOU'RE EXPERIENCING THE EXACT
SAME THINGS THAT YOUR OFFICERS ARE, EVERY DAY.
—CHIEF JIM BURACK

personnel decision they make. You learn the personal connections between aggrieved police officers and politicians. You go into a city council meeting and suddenly take a beating over something totally unrelated to the subject at hand, and you find out that Officer So-and-So was friends with Councilman So-and-So, and this is 'get-even' time."

Chief Burack agreed that running a small police department is not necessarily easier in every way than running a large department. "A small-agency chief needs to bring a breadth of skills to the table, because there's an expectation that you'll be a working chief," he said. "We're regularly on the street. We write traffic tickets, we go out on patrol. And you get direct contact with people and their complaints; you don't have a lot of insulation in the bureaucracy. As a small agency chief, you have to be very responsive. If you're a good small-agency chief, you're in tune with what's happening at the retail level. So it's much less likely that you'll get blindsided by anything, because you're experiencing the exact same things that your officers are, every day."

One obvious advantage of being a small-agency chief, Burack added, is that "you have the ability to turn the organization a lot more quickly than you do in a big organization. And with all those contacts you make in the community, it builds your credibility, so it's like money in the bank when there's an initiative you want to take the lead on, and you can get the community support for it."

In fact, Flynn said, "Often you see people from larger jurisdictions crash and burn when they try to take over a small agency, because they're used to having very large bureaucracies to which they can delegate lots of their work. They find themselves in a smaller agency in which much is expected of them personally, and there's no place to take it."

Urban vs. Suburban Policing

Flynn also drew a distinction between urban and suburban departments. "If you want to be leading an urban agency some-day, it's good to have your street and frontline-supervision experience in an urban agency," he said. "The urban cop culture is different from the suburban cop culture, given its intensity, its diversity, given the fact that urban departments often have difficult political histories. I think it's good to have an understanding of that." Sometimes suburban officers have a perspective that does not translate well into urban agencies, he said—a perspective that may be characterized as "We have all the toys, we have all the equipment, we're a service department, we answer all the calls for service, we don't exercise a lot of discretion." And some-times, suburban police "are somewhat suspicious of their urban brethren," he said. "They think that city cops are corrupt, they're brutal." Having experience in an urban department gives you the first-hand knowledge that those stereotypes are wrong, and that the large majority of officers want to do the right thing, he indicated. In sum, Flynn said, "I think you need to be able to speak to the experience of the people for whom you're responsible."

Steel Yourself for the Selection Process

Chiefs said that the process of being considered for a position as police chief is often very difficult. "Understand the selection pro-cess has become a brutal experience in many locations, even if you get the job," Stephens said. "The news media, unions, special-interest groups, and politicians who aren't even involved in the decision may weigh in publicly with their views of your suitability for the position." Strong preparation can help a candidate sur-vive the process, Stephens indicated. "Read the charter, read the contract, know what the critical policies are, and understand the issues you face in the department, the community, the political arena and the ongoing or recent controversies," he advised.

"Look into your own closet," McNeilly said. "There is nothing that you do in your personal life that isn't public record," he said, "and you have to be prepared for that. And be aware that if the forces that oppose you can't find anything, they will make it up. It's not easy to disprove a lie or straighten out the record once an accusation has been made."

When an Offer Is on the Table

The subject of terms of employment is covered in PERF's publication, *Command Performance: Career Guide for Police Executives.* But it deserves attention here as well. Some chiefs interviewed for this book are employed under a contact, others under an employment letter. (See question 7 in "Police Chief Compensation Packages 2009," an appendix to this book.) A few serve at the pleasure of their bosses. Some have worked under various employment arrangements. Some chiefs favor a contract; most expressed ambivalence about the means by which their terms of employment are prescribed.

But there was strong agreement that the time to anticipate needs and problems that you might encounter down the road, and the time to get them addressed, is when you are negotiating for the position.

Flynn was one of the police executives who said that often, it doesn't matter whether a chief works under a contract, an employment letter, or at the pleasure of the mayor or city manager. But whatever type of employment agreement is pursued, he advised, chiefs should make certain that all areas of concern are addressed at the outset. "You only have one bite at the apple," he observed.

Esserman is a strong believer in having a contract. "You can't negotiate anything if don't have a contract," he said. "You'd better get what you want and what you know you'll need regarding salary, benefits, and a car for personal and business use." If those issues are not nailed down, they are likely to become bones of contention at some point in a chief's tenure, he warned.

For example, given that a chief is always on call, it is not unusual to find chiefs having to respond to emergencies and go to work on their days off. That is why the use of a department vehicle and cell phone for business or private use is an accepted policy for chiefs. But it must be agreed upon from the beginning, and put into writing. "Get what you want before you take the job," Esserman said. "It's when you are courting that you can get it."

Another item to work out is the extent to which a chief will be reimbursed for the costs of attending professional development meetings and seminars, chiefs said.

A contract can provide chiefs with a degree of security in a job known for uncertainty. For example, one chief said that his current five-year contract guarantees him three years of employment (absent misconduct), after which the city has the option to retain him for the remaining two years. However, if city officials decide not to exercise the extension option, the city still has to pay the chief for the final two years of the contract.

But Kerlikowske said he does not favor employment contracts for chiefs. "That just gives you severance benefits if you are forced out," he said. Instead, he believes the police chief position should be an "at-will" appointment.

Stephens said that "one of the most important issues to negotiate is the ability to make the final decisions on command staff choices. I would not accept a position where the mayor appoints key command-level personnel," he said.

Bratton said that as part of his employment agreement, he negotiates bringing in outside experts on a consulting basis to vet prospective command staffers and to carry out a "cultural diagnostic—an analysis of the culture of the organization that I am going into." Such an analysis, which Bratton called "a CAT scan," can uncover serious problems in the way a department's officers function, he said.

Watson said that he hired a lawyer to help in negotiating his employment contract. The negotiations covered salary; benefits, including disability and health insurance and use of a city vehicle; and terms for dismissal and severance. Watson noted that his contract also provided for an automatic one-year extension if he was not given a certain amount of advance notice regarding renewal of the contract at the end of each year.

Timoney said that when he is offered a job as chief, he negotiates with city officials to make sure they do not interfere in how he does his job. "I value what my boss says and will follow the direction he or she charts for the city. But when it comes to running the police department and making decisions, I expect no interference," Timoney said. He said he has never had a problem securing city leaders' acceptance of that condition.

Chapter 3

Making the Transition to Chief

It's a Huge Leap to the Chief's Office

Most incoming chiefs arrive in the chief's office with extensive experience acquired after years of service at the command level. Nevertheless, that won't prepare you for the "huge leap" to the chief's office, as Kerlikowske put it.

For one thing, "you have to have so much energy in this job," Kerlikowske observed. "It's very demanding. You have to be the first one there in the morning and the last one out at night." Furthermore, "there's a certain distance between chiefs and troops, and even if you have served on a command staff, you don't get the opportunity to learn all that you need to know" before you make the leap to chief, Kerlikowske added.

However, even if first-time chiefs do not have 100 percent of the preparation they need, most have about 80 percent, which is enough if you want the job and are willing to spend time learning and seeing how things work, Kerlikowske added.

> YOU HAVE TO HAVE SO MUCH ENERGY IN THIS JOB.
> IT'S VERY DEMANDING. YOU HAVE TO BE
> THE FIRST ONE THERE IN THE MORNING AND
> THE LAST ONE OUT AT NIGHT.
> **—CHIEF GIL KERLIKOWSKE**

Trust, But Verify

Chiefs said it is important to "trust, but verify" when people tell you what to expect in a new job. It is important to listen to what people tell you, chiefs said, but you also need to "get in there and get a feel for the situation for yourself," as one chief said.

A chief is never going to arrive at a department on his or her first day with a complete picture of the challenges ahead, Watson said. Despite Watson's efforts to gain insight into the workings of the Cambridge department, "the officials I spoke with couldn't tell me everything that was wrong in the department," he said.

"You're never going to get the full story," Hurtt said. "For one thing, your new bosses may not tell you about an existing problem because then they will have to pay to get it fixed." By way of example, Hurtt said that in one department where he served as chief, no one told him that there was no plan in place to come up with funds that would be needed to purchase new radios.

When an Insider Becomes Chief

Chief Bully-Cummings, who joined the Detroit Police Department at age 19 and worked her way up to the chief's job in 2003, said that the obvious advantage of being promoted from within is that "I have an understanding of the people in the department and the community. I don't need that lead time to develop those types of relationships."

But being promoted from within can be tricky, Cline said. When he received the top job in Chicago after serving more than three decades within the department, his promotion changed the nature of his professional interactions with longtime colleagues who, having worked alongside him for years, now worked for him. While this transition requires some adjustment, it is not necessarily

> YOU'RE NEVER GOING TO GET THE FULL STORY [ABOUT WHAT TO EXPECT IN A NEW JOB]. FOR ONE THING, YOUR NEW BOSSES MAY NOT TELL YOU ABOUT AN EXISTING PROBLEM BECAUSE THEN THEY WILL HAVE TO PAY TO GET IT FIXED.
> —CHIEF HAROLD HURTT

> [ON COMPLAINTS THAT SURFACE WHEN A CHIEF
> MOVES AGAINST NON-PERFORMING EMPLOYEES]
> I ALWAYS SAY THAT IF YOU WANTED EVERYONE TO LIKE
> YOU, YOU SHOULD HAVE BECOME A CIRCUS CLOWN,
> NOT A POLICE SUPERVISOR.
> **—SUPERINTENDENT PHIL CLINE**

a friendship-ender, he said. "Your friends that you made when you came up on the job will understand that."

Nevertheless, Cline noted that he had to make decisions that were not well received by former colleagues. "I had to move people to positions that they didn't approve of, and I lost friends," he said. "You have to explain to them that it's business. I always say that if you wanted everyone to like you, you should have become a circus clown, not a police supervisor." And objections from the non-performers on the force probably should be taken as indicators of the merits of a decision, he said. "If the dogs don't like you, you're probably doing OK," Cline said.

Another former Chicago Police Superintendent agreed. "Friendship is one thing," said Terry Hillard, who competed against a friend for the chief's job. "The job of police chief is another thing. This job is about business. If you can keep those two things separate, you're going to make it." Hillard acknowledged that when he took the top job in Chicago, "it took about three months for it to sink in" that he was now running the department where he began his law enforcement career. Asked how he managed the transition from a command position to chief, Hillard said, "I hit the ground running and went out to all the police districts, all watches, and talked to them. I told them about myself and said this was going to be a team effort. I told them what I expected and where I wanted to go."

> [ON TAKING OVER AS POLICE CHIEF]
> I HIT THE GROUND RUNNING AND WENT OUT TO ALL THE
> POLICE DISTRICTS, ALL WATCHES, AND TALKED TO THEM.
> I TOLD THEM ABOUT MYSELF AND SAID THIS WAS GOING
> TO BE A TEAM EFFORT. I TOLD THEM WHAT I EXPECTED
> AND WHERE I WANTED TO GO."
> **—SUPERINTENDENT TERRY HILLARD**

For the Outsider Chief: Adjusting to the Culture of the Organization

Chiefs taking over in a new department where they have not worked before face different challenges, starting with adjusting to a different police culture. In fact, the central difference between police departments is the difference in "the culture of the organizations," said Kerlikowske, who has served in six departments, including four in the top position. For example, he recalled one time when a city council member asked him during an interview for the chief's job, "What do you think of that community policing stuff?" It was clear that the council member did not have a high opinion of community policing.

Stephens said that a new chief coming from outside a department should also expect to revisit controversial issues within the department, some of which may have been matters of dispute for years, such as educational policies for promotion, residency requirements, uniforms, and transfers.

Hurtt, who has served as chief in three departments, said that one department was particularly challenging to him because it had a strong history of thinking that "change is something that comes only when something breaks or there is a disaster." He made the adjustment and had a number of successes—"but not without bumps and bruises," he added.

One advantage for an outsider is the hope that employees have for a fresh start. Flynn observed, "In police culture, mistakes can follow you around your whole career. With an outsider chief, it's a second chance for everybody, and a strong incentive to back up the new chief's agenda. If you're that new chief, you get the advantage of their enthusiasm and the advantage that accrues to you when none of the inside cliques can claim you as one of their own."

WITH AN OUTSIDER CHIEF, IT'S A SECOND CHANCE FOR EVERYBODY, AND A STRONG INCENTIVE TO BACK UP THE NEW CHIEF'S AGENDA. IF YOU'RE THAT NEW CHIEF, YOU GET THE ADVANTAGE OF THEIR ENTHUSIASM AND THE ADVANTAGE THAT ACCRUES TO YOU WHEN NONE OF THE INSIDE CLIQUES CAN CLAIM YOU AS ONE OF THEIR OWN.
—CHIEF ED FLYNN

Lansdowne, who became chief in San Diego after serving as chief in Richmond and San Jose, Calif., agreed that there are some advantages to coming in as an outsider. "The good thing about it is that you have no baggage that you have to worry about, no prior commitments to people. You start new and can pretty much build your own organization."

A chief whose predecessor had a successful tenure will likely have a different experience than one whose predecessor is regarded as having failed in his mission, Myers noted. If the previous chief was successful, the new chief may benefit by inheriting a well-run department. But the achievements of the predecessor raise the bar for the new chief's performance. "It's easier to be considered a success if your predecessor was a less-than-stellar performer," Myers said.

Chiefs also will find cultural differences associated with the size of the department they serve as chief. As one chief said, "The smaller the department, the more the town leaders are certain they know best how to do the job."

Hit the Ground Running with Your Change Mission

Chiefs should arrive at their new job with a vision for their department and a concept of what they need to do to achieve that vision. "A good leader makes it clear what his or her vision is, and attracts those who believe in that vision to the leadership team," said Bully-Cummings.

A new chief should carry out an assessment of the strengths and weaknesses of the department, and in so doing, "listen to what the department personnel want," Kerlikowske said. "You've got to understand where you are weak, what your department does not do well," he emphasized.

Hurtt advised to strike fast, within the first 12 to 18 months, to effect change. Timoney said that in his view, the window for change is even smaller than that. "New chiefs have about a three-month window," he said. "That's when your bosses are anticipating change, and are most likely to accept it." Any controversial personnel or policy changes should be implemented quickly—and unilaterally, in Timoney's view. "That approach has worked for me every single time," Timoney said. "Put the policy out, and then go to roll call and defend it."

By way of example, Timoney said that when he took over as chief in one city, he took away officers' blackjacks and gave them mace instead. The department was the last major department in the country that used blackjacks, he said, and the change was not a popular one. "I went to roll call, explained the change, and said 'Anyone object?'" Timoney recalled. His way of explaining the reasoning for the change was to tell the officers, "Your job is to clean up the quality of life; mine is to keep you out of trouble."

Kunkle said that sometimes the pressure to move fast comes from within the department. When he took over in one city, he knew there would be a great deal of pressure from elected officials and the news media to make changes, particularly to reduce serious crime. "I found that almost everything I touched in those early days and months needed attention, and the staff knew it," Kunkle said. "My initial goal had been to spend some time listening, and resist making changes for perhaps three months after starting. But I found that the officers were seeking leadership and adjustments right away."

At the same time, Lansdowne advised outsiders to avoid making any precipitous changes unless they are taking over a department that is in crisis. "You've got to go in slow," he said. "You need time to build relationships with the officers and the community and the council before you make changes in the process."

A Few Words of Caution about Change

Be tough, confident, and decisive in your role as change agent, and get moving on your plans for change early in your administration, chiefs advise. But "be thoughtful about the department's history and weigh the risks," Berkow added.

Ramsey noted that new chiefs need to be especially careful when they take the top job in a department that is already considered a success. "I think that a chief taking over a department with a history of solid leadership and a good reputation must be careful, because any changes he or she may feel are necessary will not be accepted readily by the political leadership or the rank and file," he said. "They believe they are already at the top of their game."

"In a situation where a department is having issues," Ramsey continued, "change is easier. You can implement your ideas and bring in talented people without a lot of political interference."

Sometimes, seemingly minor changes can create trouble that undermine efforts to make more important reforms, chiefs warned. One chief described a colleague's decision to change a department's traditional white hats to blue hats, which brought a tremendous backlash from the troops. In another department, a new chief with a preference for two patches on uniform sleeves decided against changing the existing one-patch policy when it became clear that "you raise the issue of patches in that department at great risk."

Chiefs also advised their colleagues not to risk failure by taking on too much at one time. Chiefs should pick carefully what they are going to do and set their sights on achieving one goal at a time, Kerlikowske said. "If you try to take on too much, you're going to exhaust yourself and fail at all your goals."

Hurtt agreed. "Fight one battle at a time," he said. Then he quipped, "That would be fine if only the opposition did the same thing."

Rallying Your Officers in Support of Your Vision and Mission

Regardless of what a chief sees as his or her mission, the strategy for achieving that mission "can't work unless the troops on the street do it," Cline noted. "The big thing is getting everybody moving in the same direction."

If you can succeed in getting an entire department to share your vision, it can be a tremendous force for change. Cline said that he spent time discussing the department's violent crime strategy with command and non-command staff members, and "people would tell me they never saw the department with as singular a mission. They all knew what was going on, and they all talked to each other and were sharing information."

Chiefs need to create an environment that encourages department personnel to give them feedback on their plans, Ramsey added. "And you need to be open and listen to what they have to say," he added. "The troops will do what you say, even if they know you're wrong. If you are too full of yourself and create an environment where your employees are afraid to speak up, you won't get honest feedback."

The process of developing a vision for the department not only helps new chiefs plan where they want to take the department, it also can be the first step toward improving communications between the chief and his or her personnel, Watson said. He said that in formulating his plan, he reached down into the department to identify "some of the things that they wanted to see happen." By incorporating officers' ideas in the plan—creation of a stress unit, peer counseling, availability of a psychologist, for example—the lines of communication began to open.

Cline added that chiefs should continue to solicit input from officers as their plans for the department are implemented. For a ground-up view, Cline rode with officers every Friday night. "That way, you get to see how the programs that you think work so well *actually* work," he said.

Cline found that the success that the Chicago Police Department experienced with a violent crime initiative helped to rally front-line officers behind the plan. "Everybody wants to be a part of a winning team," he said. "The ones who normally sit in the middle of the road start seeing some success and they jump on board."

Of course, a chief's initial message to his or her troops depends on the issues the department is facing. When Ramsey arrived at the Washington, D.C. Metropolitan Police Department, he said he found "a largely troubled department, where there were many good people trapped in a very bad set of circumstances." The department lacked policies, procedures, and leadership from the chief and senior staff, and the department leaders had allowed training to "slip to a point where the officers were crying for training that the department was not providing."

Ramsey said the critical concern to him was that "the pride was gone," so his first order of business became reestablishing officers' pride in their department. He made a priority of making himself very accessible to personnel inside the department. Outside the department, where there was a great deal of criticism of the police, Ramsey said he aimed at "taking the focus off of the department and putting it on me" in order to give officers some relief.

Ramsey convened a meeting of all members of the department at DAR Constitution Hall, a landmark building near the White House. Speaking before several thousand officers, Ramsey delivered a PowerPoint presentation in which he explained what he had identified as the department's strengths and weaknesses, and laid out his five-year plan for making improvements. "I did this," he said, "because I wanted to establish for them my vision for the

I WOULD RATHER DEVOTE ENERGY TO GETTING
OFFICERS TO WEAR BULLET-RESISTANT VESTS THAN
ALIENATING THEM OVER FINDING FAULT BECAUSE
THEY DIDN'T WEAR THEIR HAT OR THEY ACCEPTED
A CUP OF COFFEE FROM A MERCHANT.
—CHIEF HAROLD HURTT

department—and let them know that I didn't think that things in the department were *all* wrong."

After the presentation, Ramsey said he answered questions for two to three hours, answering every question. "I told them that the department had let them down, that I would give them the equipment and other resources that they needed to do their jobs, and that then I would hold their feet to the fire with respect to their performance," Ramsey said.

Stephens agreed that new chiefs should go out of their way to make themselves accessible to employees. "Attend roll calls, visit work sites, go to social events where officers go," he said. "You can get to know a lot of people, even by taking the time to have those brief hallway conversations."

The Message on Expectations— and Police Misconduct

Early in their administrations, chiefs must set standards for their officers' performance and communicate their intention to enforce those standards, chiefs said. Failure to do this undermines officers' desire to work and contributes to misconduct, they said.

Most of the chiefs interviewed for this book have had experience with the problem of police misconduct. Several chiefs have made their reputations turning around departments plagued by corruption or other misconduct. All of the chiefs said that intolerance of police misconduct is an absolute in their administrations.

Hurtt said that when he took over as chief in one city, he found officers who "wanted leaders they could respect." He said he needed to take disciplinary actions at that department that would never have been necessary in the other departments where

> INTEGRITY HAS TO BE THE COIN OF THE REALM.
> AS CHIEF, YOU NEED TO PRACTICE WHAT YOU
> PREACH AND TELL YOUR COPS THAT IT IS A PRIVILEGE
> TO SERVE IN THE DEPARTMENT, NOT A RIGHT.
> **—COLONEL DEAN ESSERMAN**

he had served as chief, because the officers in the other departments knew what was expected of them. For example, Hurtt said he made certain that his troops understood that he was not going to promote officers who had been the subject of citizen complaints that were sustained.

At the same time, he said that chiefs need to be reasonable in their expectations and pick their battles. "I would rather devote energy to getting officers to wear bullet-resistant vests than alienating them over finding fault because they didn't wear their hat or they accepted a cup of coffee from a merchant," Hurtt said.

(In fact, Hurtt faced a "no confidence" vote when he required officers to wear bullet-resistant vests. But the issue soon dissipated when a veteran officer was shot in the chest and was saved by the vest.)

Communicating the Rules

Preventing officer misconduct requires a clearly articulated set of core values and a commitment to communicate, and enforce adherence to, those values. "Integrity has to be the coin of the realm," Esserman said. "As chief, you need to practice what you preach and tell your cops that it is a privilege to serve in the department, not a right."

Intolerance for misconduct and corruption, Superintendent Hillard said, "is something that you have to talk about day-in and day-out, and not just at the top levels, but at roll call, so the message goes all the way down the ranks." Because there will always be rule-breakers, no matter how clearly the rules are defined and enforced, major departments "can expect to be hit with some major incident of corruption every three or four years," Hillard said. "But I think that if you are out in front of it, and when it

> I GIVE ALL [MY NEW OFFICERS] THE SAME SERMON:
> "YOU CAN MAKE MISTAKES HERE, BUT YOU CAN'T LIE,
> AND YOU CAN'T BE DISHONEST. IT'S A TOUGH JOB,
> BUT I WANT YOU TO SUCCEED, AND YOU WOULDN'T
> BE HERE IF I DIDN'T THINK YOU CAN SUCCEED."
> **—CHIEF CHARLIE DEANE**

happens, you do your investigation quickly, that sends a message to the old and young police officers that you mean business," he added.

Deane has made it a practice to interview everyone who is hired by the Prince William County Police Department. "In practice, it's pretty much a 'done deal' by the time it gets to me, but I want to meet them and tell them what the rules are," he said. "I give them all the same sermon: 'You can make mistakes here, but you can't lie, and you can't be dishonest. It's a tough job, but I want you to succeed, and you wouldn't be here if I didn't think you can succeed.'"

Enforcing the Rules

Chiefs offered a number of suggestions for letting officers know that rules against misconduct will be enforced. "I always have put strong people in the Internal Affairs Division, people who do not have IAD backgrounds. And then I surround them with a good team," Esserman said.

"I'm death on police misconduct and on police officers who lie," said Hegerty, who was confronted with increasing incidents involving police misconduct when she took over the top job. "Once a police officer has been found to have lied, he or she has no credibility."

Sometimes, taking a hard line on misconduct not only involves showing officers that the chief means business, but also convincing local elected officials that the issue is a priority for the chief, and that the chief knows how to play hardball. Hegerty faced a crisis involving the brutal beating of a man by off-duty officers. Hegerty said she studied the backgrounds of the officers involved, and concluded that several of them never should have been allowed on the force. So she began "inserting" herself into the hiring and promotions process, even though it was under the authority of a Fire and Police Commission. She conducted her own investigations of candidates and sent recommendations to the commission.

When the commission resisted, "I told them that if I'm going to be responsible for these people and their behaviors, I want to have some input into it," Hegerty said. "So I will send my letter, either recommending or not recommending, and if for some reason you hire this person over my objection and they tarnish the badge, I will produce the letter publicly and you can deal with the results. This, of course, got their attention, and now they take my objections seriously."

Because of the beating incident scandal, Hegerty also was able to push through an Employee Intervention Program, as well as a requirement that candidates be subjected to psychological investigations.

Get Out Front and 'Fess Up
When There's a Problem . . . and Apologize

Hillard said that when a police officer violates the law, the chief's plan should be to get out in front of the issue by calling a press conference and announcing, "We are going to investigate this, and if the officer was wrong, we are going to admit that he was wrong." And if the investigation substantiates the charges, the chief should apologize, Hillard emphasized. "Those two little words— 'We're sorry'—go far in a community that has been harmed by the

> I TOLD [THE POLICE COMMISSION] THAT IF I'M GOING TO BE RESPONSIBLE FOR [NEW HIRES] AND THEIR BEHAVIORS, I WANT TO HAVE SOME INPUT INTO IT. SO I WILL SEND MY LETTER, EITHER RECOMMENDING OR NOT RECOMMENDING, AND IF FOR SOME REASON YOU HIRE THIS PERSON OVER MY OBJECTION AND THEY TARNISH THE BADGE, I WILL PRODUCE THE LETTER PUBLICLY AND YOU CAN DEAL WITH THE RESULTS. THIS, OF COURSE, GOT THEIR ATTENTION, AND NOW THEY TAKE MY OBJECTIONS SERIOUSLY.
> —RETIRED CHIEF NAN HEGERTY

inappropriate actions of police officers," he said. "When you mess up, you 'fess up, and clean up. And make sure that the cleanup is a comprehensive process so you can make sure this won't happen again."

Other chiefs agreed about the need to confront misconduct openly, rather than trying to sweep it under a rug. Chief Hanson said that when she fired an officer for lying, she convened a department-wide meeting to explain her decision and to reiterate her message that misconduct would not be tolerated.

Esserman said when an investigation results in serious discipline, he holds a press conference. "We stand together and say, 'We clean up our own. We take no pride in this, but we are not going to have someone else clean it up.'"

Intolerance of misconduct does not mean intolerance of honest mistakes, chiefs said. Watson urged chiefs to use a light hand when disciplining officers who make good-faith mistakes. Counseling sometimes is a better alternative to harsh discipline, he said.

Hurtt cited a case in which an officer had a high number of Taser discharges. Hurtt said he gave the officer a video camera to record his interactions with subjects in the field. After that, he said, the officer's use of the Taser stopped.

Likewise, Hillard said that when he briefed officers on his disciplinary policy, he sometimes invoked their experience as parents. "How many of you have kids?" he asked. "When they make mistakes, do you discipline them every time? No. So when you make an honest mistake, I'm going to help you. If you make a criminal mistake, I'm going to come after you."

Kunkle said that under his system of discipline, if an act of misconduct requires punishment greater than a reprimand, "I get the case." And he has taken the position that if a case of misconduct is referred to him, he wants to meet with the officer personally before deciding what sanction to impose. That helps him to

---

WHEN YOU MESS UP, YOU 'FESS UP, AND CLEAN UP.
AND MAKE SURE THAT THE CLEANUP IS A
COMPREHENSIVE PROCESS SO YOU CAN MAKE SURE
THIS WON'T HAPPEN AGAIN.
—SUPERINTENDENT TERRY HILLARD

CHOOSE SOMEONE [TO HEAD INTERNAL AFFAIRS]
WHO WON'T BACK DOWN FROM ANYONE WHEN
IT COMES TO DEALING WITH CORRUPTION.
—FORMER SUPERINTENDENT TERRY HILLARD

assess the fine points of balancing punishment and guidance in each case.

Once an officer has been disciplined, Olson said, he believes that the incident should take its place in history and everyone should move on. He said that there should be no continuing "vindictiveness" toward the officer and no retaliatory action beyond the disciplinary sanction imposed. "Pay your dues and it's over; it's done," he said.

Chiefs advised their colleagues to select someone they trust and in whom they have confidence to head their internal affairs units.

"Choose someone who won't back down from anyone when it comes to dealing with corruption," Hillard said.

"Find someone who is honest and is respected within the department," Olson said—"someone you trust and who wants the job. You can train them to do the rest."

Timoney said that the head of an internal affairs unit also should be skilled in working with state and federal agencies that may have to be called upon in conjunction with an investigation.

Your Officers Will Be Watching You

In the end, chiefs said, a new chief should keep in mind that actions speak louder than words when you are trying to gain the confidence of your officers.

"While it's important for a new chief to talk about philosophy, integrity, and his or her plans to maintain an open-door policy with personnel in the first several months of the new administration, understand that what will make the most difference is not what is said but what is done," Stephens said.

For example, officers will watch carefully to see how a new chief handles the first officer-involved shooting or questionable pursuit and any associated disciplinary decisions. How a chief handles these early cases can set a standard of what officers expect to happen, or not happen, in future cases. This can have an impact on officers' performance, their opinions about the department, and the news media's view of the agency.

Chiefs should spend time with their officers out in the streets in order to establish a rapport with them, experienced chiefs said. Time spent with the officers can also help a chief to identify ways of making officers' jobs safer and more productive.

Sometimes small things can make a big difference in how officers perceive the chief's interest in their well-being. Cline said that under a previous chief, officers were required to wear a hat that they found necessary to remove while riding in their squad cars. However, they were required to put the hat on every time they got out of their cars on a stop; failure to do so could result in discipline. Some officers were choosing to risk discipline rather than wear their hats. "I was out on street and I saw the problem," Cline said. "In order to put their hats on, officers had to take their eyes off of the person they had stopped. So I approved a baseball cap that they could wear inside the car."

Timoney said that he lives by the philosophy of "not asking my officers to do anything I wouldn't do myself." That includes being on the front lines with them when there is a critical situation. A major drawback of that approach is that "you can't see the forest for the trees," he acknowledged. "But if you are asking your officers to use enormous restraint, you can't ask them to do it by themselves." Being out on the front line with his officers gives him the opportunity to intervene to "help control their emotions" when they are confronted with difficult situations, he said.

A Few Final Observations and Advice for the Transitioning Chief

Chiefs had a few final observations and words of advice for the transitioning chief: Reach out to trusted colleagues for advice in making the hard decisions. Manage your time effectively. And don't lose sight of the big picture.

A Circle of Trusted Advisors

Some chiefs spoke of the importance of having trusted confidants within and outside the department to whom they turn for advice.

(At the same time, Hegerty cautioned chiefs to be sensitive to the idea that having an informal group of advisors can engender resentment among command staff members.)

Ramsey said he has benefited from having a small circle of trusted individuals from outside the department who can be tapped for advice. For example, in preparing for a public rally which drew thousands of protestors to Washington, D.C., Ramsey said he found himself in disagreement with department special operations officials. "Special operations had a plan that I didn't think was right. I made changes that were not received well, because it was a departure from what they were accustomed to." To gain a better perspective, Ramsey said, he sat down with a former chief who had been in the department when thousands of protesters were arrested during an anti-war demonstration. The former chief reviewed and concurred with Ramsey's decision, "and that raised my confidence to go through with my plan, which proved to be a success," he said. Moreover, the former chief, who has a broad political base in the city, was a tremendous asset in garnering support for Ramsey's actions among community leaders.

Developing a cadre of individuals outside the department whom you can turn to for advice is "a good leadership practice—even in small departments," said Kerlikowske.

On Time Management

Managing your time can be one of the more difficult aspects of adjusting to the role of chief, because each chief needs to find his or her own pattern that works.

Bratton indicated that he is not impressed by people who work extremely long hours. "Some people talk about how difficult the job of police chief is," he said. "I don't. If you think it's too tough, get out of it. It is what it is, and I enjoy it. You should never portray your job, or the position of police chief in general, or the profession of policing, in a negative light. We all know people who talk about how hard they're working—80 hours a week, or they were up til 3 a.m. working on something, or they didn't get home at all last night. Anyone who works that hard, I have concerns about. I work hard, but I'm not killing myself, and part of the reason is that I surround myself with a lot of people who also work hard, and who work in a shared way, sharing the load."

Still, making the transition to the position of chief can pose new challenges in terms of time management. Cline said that for

SOME PEOPLE TALK ABOUT HOW DIFFICULT
THE JOB OF POLICE CHIEF IS. I DON'T.
IF YOU THINK IT'S TOO TOUGH, GET OUT OF IT....
YOU SHOULD NEVER PORTRAY YOUR JOB, OR THE
POSITION OF POLICE CHIEF IN GENERAL, OR THE
PROFESSION OF POLICING, IN A NEGATIVE LIGHT.
—CHIEF WILLIAM BRATTON

him, "the hardest adjustment was no longer having time to make myself available to people I have known for years. They found that they couldn't just run up the stairs and meet with me. Your day's not your own. A lot of people don't realize that and may think that you think you're too good for them. Your schedule is so tight that if you took the time to meet with everyone who just dropped in, it would throw the rest of your day out of whack. Some people don't understand that and wonder if you've changed. Furthermore, there are hundreds of groups that would like to meet with you," Cline said, so chiefs need to find a balance between making themselves accessible and managing their own time. "The hardest thing to do is to tell people no," he said.

Lansdowne said that big-city chiefs simply need to accept that the job involves a lot of hours. His routine is to begin each day with a 5:30 a.m. meeting with night-shift lieutenants, who have a very important job, in Lansdowne's view. "I hand-pick all the lieutenants, and there are only a few who get to work the night shift," he said. "They're not assigned to the Patrol Division; they're assigned directly to me, because they're really the chiefs of police at night. So I meet with them in the morning and we run through everything that's gone on through the night. And by the time 7 o'clock rolls around, I've already had that meeting and two or three others, and I know where the problems are. I know what the press is going to hit me on, and I know what the mayor's going to want to know about. If we've got gang problems going on, for example, I know about it, and by 8 o'clock we have a plan to deal with those gang problems."

Lansdowne applies his own strong work ethic to subordinates as well. "When I got here, the captains got in at 9, left at 3, had weekends off, didn't go to community events on the weekend. Now they go to all those events. And I expect them to know as much as I do about the latest problems and what's going on. If I call them up and they don't know at least as much as I do, I make sure they get into the loop."

Does starting every day with meetings at 5:30 become a drain? "I put in a lot of time, and that might not work for everyone, but for me, I'm really uncomfortable if I don't know what's going on," Lansdowne said.

The need to set priorities can force chiefs to make difficult decisions about how they spend their time. Asked if he routinely goes out on calls involving serious or violent crime, Cline said that he used to go out on "heater cases" that generate a lot of news media attention, as well as any officer-involved shooting. However, in a city as large as Chicago, such incidents are not as rare as in small departments, and Cline had to modify his practice when he quickly discovered that "I couldn't keep up the pace the rest of the day." He decided to limit himself to going out if a police officer was injured. But he would call every officer involved in a shooting and make sure they were doing all right and were meeting with the department's Counseling Service. "You need to remember what your job is as chief," Cline said. "You can't go out on everything, and you have to trust your command staff," he cautioned.

Stay Focused on the Big Picture

Chiefs advised their colleagues to be careful not to get mired in the details of the chief's job. "If there is one lesson I've learned that chiefs need to remember, it's to stay focused on the big picture," said Kunkle. To that end, he advises his colleagues to read as much as they can, from a variety of sources, about what is going on in other police departments. Chiefs who myopically limit their attention to what is happening in their own department run the risk of plowing old ground and repeating the errors made in other departments.

Kunkle also said he finds it frustrating that lessons learned in policing are often forgotten over time, "so we end up reliving the same experience every 20 years." Kunkle urged chiefs to take a humble approach: Instead of thinking they will somehow be effective in a way that their predecessors were not, chiefs should understand that they will probably spend much of their time confronting many of the same issues that their predecessors, and their colleagues in other departments, have confronted, and should try to learn from their experiences.

Chapter 4

Developing and Empowering Your Command Team

The police chiefs who were interviewed for this book had a lot to say about building, managing, and evaluating the performance of their command staff. They emphasized that chiefs have an obligation to consult with and empower their command staff; to give the members of the staff opportunities to show what they can do; and to help command staff members develop their leadership skills.

In situations where a new chief has taken office and is allowed to make changes in his or her command staff, there is a difference of opinion about how quickly those changes should be made. Some chiefs, like John Timoney, advise making changes quickly. "You need to recognize that you were probably brought in to make changes," he said.

Others warn that chiefs need to be circumspect about shaking things up.

Chiefs generally agreed on three imperatives:

- Even if you have the opportunity to come in the door and immediately remove the existing command staff, wait until you have sufficient information to make informed choices.

- Assess the capabilities of existing command staff members and candidates for those positions before making decisions about changes.

- Solicit the opinions of knowledgeable people, but also do your own research and draw your own conclusions about whether candidates will make a good fit with your administration.

You Probably Will Be Limited in
Choosing Your Command Staff

The reality, chiefs said, is that very few chiefs are given the opportunity to build their command staff from the ground up. Constraints imposed on a chief's hiring authority under union contracts, civil service systems, or simply the prevailing politics mean that most chiefs have to "play with the hand that was dealt to you," Kunkle said. Hegerty said that the only command staff position that she had any role in filling was assistant chief. She had no authority to remove command staff members, even those who were not suited for their positions or were not performing well.

Sometimes, special circumstances give a new chief an opportunity to make big changes in an inherited command staff. Esserman said he took over a department that was under scrutiny for allegations of corruption and mismanagement, and he retired the entire command staff. Hurtt found it necessary to remove two deputy chiefs who were in conflict with each another, which gave him the opportunity to pick his own people for these posts. McNeilly said that mass retirements gave him a chance to shape his own command staff in Pittsburgh.

Dealing with Inherited Staff Conflicts

Many chiefs will find that they have inherited not only a command staff, but also the remnants of conflicts that existed between the command staff and the previous chief. This can undermine the new chief's efforts to win the confidence and cooperation of the command staff. Bully-Cummings reported that she was surprised by the level of resistance to her leadership that she encountered from command staff. She attributed the resistance to lingering fallout from the tenure of her predecessor, who she said justifiably had "come in tough" in an effort to get a grip on a troubled and highly political department.

Others will contend with resentment from command officers who competed for and lost in their bids to become chief. One chief said he had to deal with a deputy who "was hurt because he didn't get the job." The deputy made the transition and became a committed member of the command staff, this chief said, "but it took years for him to get over not getting the chief's job."

[ON THE DIFFICULTY OF WORKING WITH
COMMANDERS WHOM YOU HAVE NOT CHOSEN]
I THINK THERE WOULD HAVE BEEN MORE INCENTIVE
TO BE LOYAL TEAM PLAYERS IF THEY KNEW I HAD
MORE DISCRETION OVER APPOINTMENTS.
-CHIEF INSPECTOR KATHLEEN O'TOOLE

Former Boston Police Commissioner Kathleen O'Toole said that in retrospect, one key thing she would have changed about her experience in Boston would have been insisting on the option of recruiting some of her top commanders from outside of the organization. "At least seven members of my senior command staff competed with me for the job," she said. "In fairness, most of them were great, but a few were problematic and there were long-standing rivalries between some of them. I think there would have been more incentive to be loyal team players if they knew I had more discretion over appointments."

Another chief said that the biggest intradepartmental problem that he has encountered to date stemmed from the severely strained relationships between two of three command staff members who had competed against him and with each other for the job of chief. "There was a real fight in here to get the chief's job," he explained. "Two factions broke down into open warfare. A lot of bad blood remains between those two factions, and it has resulted in really bad police work occurring here. Everyone is taking sides, down to the patrol officer on the street. They're almost physically fighting over tactics."

A chief faced with these types of sensitive issues can seek advice from others, but in the end it may simply depend on the chief's best assessment of how to balance the personal dynamics involved. McNeilly said that when he became chief of the Pittsburgh Bureau of Police, where he started his policing career, "it created a strange situation, because the assistant chief I had been working with suddenly was working for me. I knew that I had to get things right if we were going to work well together, so I created a deputy chief position and promoted the assistant chief to that slot."

Chiefs also advised their colleagues to be prepared to receive pushback from their officers when they promote an officer of lower rank to a command staff post over more senior personnel, or make other unpopular decisions about personnel. Kunkle promoted a lieutenant to the deputy's post over several higher-ranking officers. Asked whether other department supervisors were supportive or resentful of that decision, Kunkle said there was "a little bit of both. A lot of them didn't like it, but they accepted it."

Timoney likewise gave key command staff positions to several officers who had fallen out of grace with his predecessor, much to the consternation of other officials in the department. He told his new command staff members, "You're working for me, so don't worry about it."

On Bringing in Outsiders

The majority of chiefs interviewed said it is essential that chiefs try to make a few of their own choices in building a command staff. But there are different views on whether chiefs should consider bringing in these people from outside the department, or should seek to fill these slots from among insiders.

Bratton asserted that "the best leadership team is made up of insiders and outsiders." Watson said he believes that bringing talented outsiders into a police department is good for the policing profession. Watson came in as an outsider to head the police department in Cambridge, Mass., a jurisdiction with a civil service system that he described as "designed to keep outsiders out." That posture, he said, "hurts everybody, and retards police growth." Myers, who has served as chief in five departments, said that in one of his departments, he proposed opening promotions "to everyone, both inside and outside the department, every time." Myers acknowledged that "there will always be a bias for insiders, and the officers know it. But inviting outsiders to compete for positions opens up the process."

By contrast, Esserman said his first rule of thumb regarding building a command staff is, "I travel alone. I don't bring staff with me." Esserman said that in all three of the departments where he has been chief, he could have brought in outsiders to fill command staff slots, but he always declined to do so. "I think that when you bring a team with you, you become more isolated, and I don't want to be isolated. If you bring your team with you, it's uncomfortable for the people around you, because they don't get a chance to compete for command staff positions, and it gives them the impression that you don't trust them."

[ON WHETHER TO HIRE MEMBERS OF
YOUR COMMAND STAFF FROM OUTSIDE THE DEPARTMENT]
THERE WILL ALWAYS BE A BIAS FOR INSIDERS,
AND THE OFFICERS KNOW IT. BUT INVITING OUTSIDERS
TO COMPETE FOR POSITIONS OPENS UP THE PROCESS.
-CHIEF RICK MYERS

For most chiefs, the only way to bring someone of their own choosing onto the command staff is to hire people from outside the department. Several chiefs said that they navigated around restrictions on their ability to change the existing command staff by negotiating during their own hiring process, and demanding their bosses' approval to hire experienced and talented individuals to fill non-civil service positions. Chiefs interviewed for this project reported bringing in as few as one and as many as a dozen civilians to their command staffs.

Hiring civilians for top positions can change the dynamics of the entire department. In two of the departments where he has served as chief, Flynn inherited a command staff but hired a civilian to be chief of staff and another to be the equivalent of a deputy chief. The presence of high-ranking civilians has elevated the status of other civilian employees in the department; "now civilians don't feel like eighth-class citizens," he said.

Finally, chiefs advised their colleagues to look for and be comfortable with bringing into their inner circle people who just might be smarter than they are. Esserman said he has no qualms about promoting people to supervisory posts who may be smarter or more skilled than he is. "I've learned that it's really OK to surround yourself with people who are better than you. I find out who the real leaders in the department are and promote them to command positions."

If you don't have the option of making all the changes you would like in the command staff, Kerlikowske advised "taking your time and using your influence to leverage the right people into the right jobs." Kerlikowske noted that in his experience as chief, he has never actually had to drop someone from the existing command staff, but the situation is made clear to those who have not performed well, and some have left for retirement or other assignments.

Choosing the Right People

The skills, experience, and past performance of command staff candidates will tell you whether they are capable of doing the job, but their character will provide critical insight into what kind of job they will do, chiefs said. Character traits are significant indicators of whether a candidate can be counted on to exercise good judgment. And on a practical level, character, demeanor, and values also can determine whether the chief and a command officer will be able to work together as a team.

Chiefs interviewed for this project said that integrity is the character trait that they value most highly in their command staff. "I choose people because of their integrity, not their skills," Esserman said.

Burack agreed, saying that officers of good character can be trained in the skills they are lacking, but a lack of integrity and other character flaws are insidious and difficult to remediate. "Hire for attitude; train for skills," he said.

Other character traits valued by chiefs included a passion for policing, inquisitiveness, strong personal values, and the courage to disagree with the chief. Chiefs also should look for candidates who have a good work ethic. "Is the candidate out the door at 5:00 p.m., or a hard worker who can be trusted to stick with an assignment until it is completed?" said Hanson.

Chiefs said they value loyalty—but that means commitment and loyalty to the department and the office of chief, the community, and the mission of the department, not loyalty to the chief personally. As one chief put it, "I've never told anyone who worked for me, 'Don't embarrass me.' I always say, 'Don't embarrass the department.'"

Burack said that sometimes it takes time for a commander's loyalties to become clear. A new chief should be able to expect that commanders will not be disloyal to the chief, and more importantly, commanders must be loyal to the organization and to the

---

HIRE FOR ATTITUDE; TRAIN FOR SKILLS.
–CHIEF JIM BURACK

profession, he said. "I came into a job inheriting a Number Two—who had been the acting chief and may have even been considering applying for the job permanently—and who I truly hoped would become an integral and productive member of my command team. But within a few months it became clear it was not a good fit. So I rearranged the command structure, transferring critical operational responsibilities to a new command position I established."

A strong leadership team, chiefs said, should have breadth in skills and depth in experience. Kunkle said that he looks for a command staff that complements his skills and those of other members of his leadership team. "My Number Two guy is the opposite of me," he said. "I try to have a big-picture orientation, and he is very detail-oriented and focused on achieving directives."

Several chiefs said the command staff must share the chief's vision of policing and must be compatible with his or her management style. Bratton reported that he removed the upper echelon of his command staff in one department because "they didn't share my vision; they didn't believe that they could change the crime situation in the city." Some of those who didn't make the cut in his police department, he readily acknowledged, "might thrive if put in another environment." This comment was echoed by Hanson, who said that one command staff member who did not function well under her leadership left the department and is doing well as police chief in another community.

Chiefs also said that they look for a command staff of individuals who can work together. "They don't have to like each other," Commissioner Davis said, "but they do have to function as a team." In fact, Bratton said, not all of the people he brought onto his command staff like each other, but he believes that some degree of tension and competitiveness among the command staff helps to raise the bar, improving both their individual performance and the performance of the team. "I want them to be competitive," he said.

MY NUMBER TWO GUY IS THE OPPOSITE OF ME.
I TRY TO HAVE A BIG-PICTURE ORIENTATION, AND
HE IS VERY DETAIL-ORIENTED AND FOCUSED ON
ACHIEVING DIRECTIVES.

–CHIEF DAVID KUNKLE

Several chiefs also noted that they always try to be sensitive to the issue of diversity in making command staff appointments, and to include women and minorities on the team.

Take Some Time to Know Your Candidates

Chiefs said it is important to take as much time as you reasonably can to get to know the capabilities of your senior staff members before you make decisions about the makeup of that staff. And most said it is a mistake to make wholesale changes too quickly. "I never came in and cleaned house with the command staff," Olson said. Ramsey agreed. "I don't believe in going in and chucking everyone," he said.

The first two or three command staff choices in particular are very critical to a new chief, Stephens observed. "Learn about who your choices really are and how they are perceived in the department and the community," he said. "It takes a while to sort out the capabilities of some people."

How long you have to deliberate will depend on a number of factors, some of which may be beyond your control. But chiefs said the important thing is to take as much time as prevailing conditions permit. Chiefs interviewed for this book said that they took from six weeks to six months to organize their command staffs.

Bratton has an interesting approach; he said he picks his senior leadership team "very early" in his administration, and "then engages them in picking the other leaders" for the command staff.

In terms of choosing a command staff, there are advantages and disadvantages to taking the chief's job as an outsider, as opposed to rising through the ranks to the top position, chiefs said. The advantage of coming in from the outside is that you can assess the capabilities of the existing leaders in a neutral manner, Kerlikowske said. But the drawback is that you have no personal knowledge of their strengths and weaknesses, and you need to rely at least in part on the knowledge of others who may not be as objective. Police departments are "cliquish," Flynn said, and members may attempt to use a new chief's lack of knowledge about department personnel to their own advantage. "People are going to represent their rivals in a way that may not be good information for you," he said.

Evaluating Candidates' Strengths and Weaknesses

To assess the qualifications of command staff members or candidates, several chiefs said that they ask for resumes and then follow up with one-on-one interviews. Flynn said that during interviews he invites staff members to describe themselves and to share their views of the department. That way, he also gets "a mini-history of the department and insight into what the issues are."

Even though the interview process can take a few months, it has the advantage of allowing new chiefs to draw their own conclusions based upon what they hear directly from the candidates, rather than what other people say about them, Flynn said.

The chief's credibility is on the line when command appointments are made, Flynn added. "More time means better decisions," he said. "If you're an outsider, everybody's on their best behavior at first. With time, they eventually tell you who they really are. Believe them."

Berkow said he asks command staff members to respond to a confidential questionnaire in which they are asked to identify "three reasons that you love working here and three things you would change if you had the opportunity." He said the answers give him insight into problems within the department—as well as a list of items of concern to personnel, from which he can choose "easy wins" to act on, helping him gain the confidence and support of his new staff.

Two chiefs said that they did not make any command staff changes for six months after they became chief. Esserman said he used this time interviewing candidates and "spending time out in the field seeing who the real leaders are, who the officers respect, and who I share common values with." Ramsey took a page from corporate hiring practices and applied process-mapping techniques to document in detail the specific roles and responsibilities of command staff assignments. And he asked all command staffers to write essays, which he said "helped me to get perspective on how they think."

Like Esserman, Ramsey looked at how his command staff performed in the field, putting potential commanders in charge of substations "to see what they could do," and giving them surprise visits. Daily crime briefings also gave Ramsey a chance to assess "how commanders responded to challenges, and how much of a grasp they had on what was going on their districts."

Ramsey said he concluded from the essays that some command staff members did not see themselves as leaders. And what he discovered by looking at their performance in the field was that many were not familiar with their local crime situations.

Timoney said that he also follows a command staff selection process that involves reviewing resumes, researching candidates' "pedigrees," and conducting interviews. He arrives at a new department knowing that he is going to make changes, and moves quickly to take a look at his command staff and decide for himself who will stay on and who will not be on the new team.

Timoney said that in selecting candidates that he will interview, he "tries to be as inclusive as possible," searching not only among acknowledged performers, but also among personnel who might not have made the grade under the previous administration. This broad reach is good strategy, he said, "because you will find a gem every once in a while." By way of example, Timoney said he found several potential leaders in the night command in one department where he served as chief. The night command, he explained, was made up largely of officers who for one reason or another had "just run afoul of the previous administration."

"I chose four or five people to come out of the dungeon for pretty important positions," Timoney said, including a "brilliant" captain who was put in charge of public relations.

Reach Out for Advice

While the chief has to make the final call, several chiefs said that they look for input from both sworn and civilian personnel to inform their command staff decisions. And many said that they also look for input from the community.

Reaching out broadly for advice from all ranks regarding command staff decisions not only improves the quality of the decision, but gives people who participate in the process a stake in the outcome. Hillard said he met for 90 minutes with non-supervisory personnel and gave them an opportunity to share their concerns.

Respect from fellow officers and the community, chiefs said, is a strong indicator of a candidate's potential performance as a leader. And consulting with community leaders who know the command staff candidates gives a chief the opportunity to gain insight into how his or her choices of department leaders will be viewed.

Dealing with Non-Performers

Despite chiefs' best efforts to make well-informed decisions about their command staff, most can expect to be faced at some point with the problem of non-performers. As Chief Myers observed, removing people from command staff posts is a lot more difficult than getting them into those positions. Kunkle added that removing non-performing command staff members is doubly difficult when they "have good hearts but don't have the skills or intellect or people skills to be effective."

When a command staff member whom you brought into the position doesn't work out, you should own up to the error and move quickly to correct it, chiefs said. "You can't be afraid to correct your mistakes when you make them," Ramsey said. "You are going to make mistakes, and you can't stress out about them."

Dealing with the problem of an inherited officer who is not living up to expectations is a problem for which there is no easy solution, chiefs say. Most chiefs said that they have been forced to handle this kind of situation through "attrition"—in other words, "parking them until they retire," in the words of Olson. Stephens said he prefers to find responsible work for non-performers that he believes they may be able to handle. If that doesn't work, he said, he moves them to some place within the department where they will have the least impact. Some chiefs say they shift non-performers to less desirable assignments, which eventually leads to their resignation. "You make life miserable for those who won't cooperate or work," one chief said.

Hegerty said that she too has tried to marginalize those who don't perform, but from a practical standpoint, exiling non-performers to the periphery of command staff activities can be difficult to do, because all jobs in a police department are important. It's a frustrating situation, she indicated. "You need folks in those critical jobs; the work has to be done," she said. "And it's unfair to

> YOU CAN'T BE AFRAID TO CORRECT YOUR MISTAKES
> WHEN YOU MAKE THEM. YOU ARE GOING TO MAKE
> MISTAKES, AND YOU CAN'T STRESS OUT ABOUT THEM.
> **–COMMISSIONER CHARLES RAMSEY**

THERE'S A FINE LINE BETWEEN
STABILITY AND STAGNATION.
-CHIEF ELLEN HANSON

the ones who do perform. They don't receive additional compensation for picking up the slack for their colleagues."

When you can remove a problem command staff member, how you handle the dismissal is of paramount importance, chiefs said. First and foremost, Ramsey said, "Always do it to their face and tell them why you are removing them. If you can't face them and articulate why they are being removed, then their removal probably is not justified. And make it clear that your action isn't personal; it's business."

Moreover, chiefs said, the problems that you had with the officer and your reasons for the removal should be well-documented.

One chief recommended that chiefs take advantage of circumstances when they make decisions that could cause trouble. For example, this chief made a point of making two potentially controversial demotions at a time when the news media were focused on election-year politics, and had less interest in police department affairs. The assistant chiefs being demoted had their own power bases, which under ordinary circumstances might have caused trouble. But the chief waited for his opportunity and then moved quickly. "I pulled the trigger before they knew what was going on," he said.

Empowering Command Staff

Chiefs said that the aim of every chief in building his or her command staff should be to develop leaders who can be trusted to carry out the chief's mission and to do the right thing. "A chief's focus always should be on making folks as good as they can be, and then recognizing them for their accomplishments," Olson said.

Developing command staff includes empowering them, chiefs said—giving them the authority to show what they can do when difficult decisions must be made. That means delegating authority

> ## DON'T UNDERESTIMATE THE ATTRACTION
> ## OF BEING ON A WINNING TEAM AS AN INCENTIVE.
> ## –CHIEF JOHN TIMONEY

and sharing power with the command staff. "You've got to give them a chance to participate," Hurtt said.

Command staff members should not stay in any one job too long, chiefs said. "When you identify talent, put them in positions where they can grow," Ramsey said. "Move them around. And let them know that they have to do the same for their people." Olson agreed. "Make sure that you move command staff through administration positions; never let them just sit," he said. Hanson said that when it comes to developing the leadership potential of your command staff, "there's a fine line between stability and stagnation."

Timoney urged his colleagues to make use of "the innate desire to be part of a winning team." For example, in one department Timoney put officers whom he had promoted to district commander ahead of others for department resources, and he let it be known within the department that the 23 captains who held the district commander posts were on his A list. "I made no bones about them being my favorites," he said. "All of a sudden, others wanted to become district commanders. Don't underestimate the attraction of being on a winning team as an incentive."

Monitoring Commanders' Performance

Giving the command staff authority to make decisions does not diminish the need for a chief to stay on top of what the command staff and their troops are doing, chiefs said. "Give them the benefit of the doubt, but verify," Olson said.

Commissioner Ramsey said that his daily 10:00 a.m. crime briefings with all assistant chiefs and his regular meetings with commanders in the Washington, D.C. Metropolitan Police Department helped to keep him current on what was happening within the community. But chiefs should not rely entirely on the information they receive from their troops, he stressed. "You can get to know your community through your commanders on the street," he explained. "But chiefs need to verify the information for themselves." Ramsey said that he stays on top of daily crime statistics, crime trends, and staffing patterns, and regularly compares statistics for the current period with numbers for the same period in the previous year or five years ago. "This gives you a real good perspective on what is going on," he said. "I know the crime in my city because every day I get information on what has happened on the streets."

Most chiefs interviewed said they use regular meetings with command staff to keep apprised of their activities. Their comments suggest that for chiefs who head large metropolitan police agencies, scheduling regular meetings with command staff arguably is a must. By contrast, in departments where the chief has a smaller span of control, chiefs may find they are able to keep in touch with the troops through a more informal approach. Chief Myers said that in Appleton, Wis., he met monthly with his captains and twice a week with his deputy chiefs. "I used to have full command staff meetings periodically, but found that those meetings weren't productive," he said. "Instead I started dropping in on the captains' and deputy chiefs' meetings." Now with a larger department in Colorado Springs, Myers and his deputy chiefs use brief daily check-ins, short weekly "tactical" meetings, and monthly "strategic" meetings with expanded command staff.

Most chiefs said that they meet weekly with command staff supervisors and at least every two weeks with all command staff. Some chiefs build their sessions with command staff around Compstat meetings.

Esserman said he does not hold separate meetings with command staff supervisors; instead, he always meets with his entire command staff, because "I want everyone to feel that they are part of the team." He said that he gives individual command staff members a great deal of freedom. "But over a period of time, I work hard to form a team—not just five or seven superstars, but a team," Esserman said. "So whatever the topic is, when we meet, we *all* meet."

Using Technology to Manage Command Staff

Lansdowne noted that chiefs can use new kinds of communications systems to stay in touch with command staff members and hold them accountable. "Technology is a wonderful thing," he said. "I get text messages all night long. If there's a major robbery, a shooting, a homicide, an officer who got injured, or we arrested someone who's a VIP or a politician or another police officer, I get text messages. And those messages go out to all the captains, so we're all up to speed. Every one of the captains gets the same information."

The text messaging issue highlights Lansdowne's approach to holding his commanders accountable. "Some complained at first; they said, 'You know, you're waking me up two or three times in the middle of the night,'" Lansdowne said. "I say, 'If you want to be a captain, you're responsible for knowing what's going on, and you need to have the information. You can't play catch-up at 9 o'clock in the morning. If your officer is hurt, or there's some major crime going on in your division, you need to deal with it *then* and make sure your lieutenants are taking care of it.'"

Building Leadership Skills in Command Staff

Nurturing the talents of command staff members, chiefs said, means giving them the opportunity to hone the skills that brought them into leadership positions in their departments. "Identify talented people," Olson said. "Then get them out of their environment. Send them places where they can learn and broaden their horizons."

"If I could do anything for people who want to be police chiefs," Kunkle said, "I'd give them the largest breadth of knowledge I could, because as officers move up through the ranks, they need to be able to see the big picture and understand how very complicated worlds operate. That's how you learn to make wise decisions and move the department in the right direction."

Kathleen O'Toole said that from the perspective of an aspiring chief, having a nurturing boss can be critically important. "I always advise young people to find great mentors," she said. "When I was 32 years old, Bill Bratton appointed me as one of his deputies in Boston's Metropolitan District Commission Police. I worked side by side with him for four years there. He gave me the opportunity to take risks, to learn how to lead and manage. He supported my professional development by encouraging me to attend programs and courses."

> SO I'D SAY TO ASPIRING POLICE CHIEFS,
> "EVEN THOUGH SOME ASSIGNMENTS CAN BE
> GRUELING OR SEEM TO BE A NUISANCE,
> IT'S GOOD TO HAVE AS MUCH DIVERSE EXPERIENCE
> UNDER YOUR BELT AS POSSIBLE."
> **—CHIEF INSPECTOR KATHLEEN O'TOOLE**

Sometimes, working for a good mentor is not glamorous, O'Toole indicated—but it is important work. "The first job Bill offered me was Deputy for Administration," she said. "I respectfully explained that I had no desire to spend my career behind a desk as an administrator. Bill then provided an incentive. He said, 'Succeed at getting good budget, HR and technology systems in place, and I'll appoint you as Deputy for Patrol Operations.' Bill did me a huge favor. The management experience I gained in that first command position served me well later. For instance, I benefited from getting a lot of labor relations experience. Bill used to send me to those labor relations meetings and I thought, 'Ugh, why do I have to go to these?' I realized years later when I walked into the commissioner's job in Boston that it was a huge advantage, having been at the table for similar discussions before. So I'd say to aspiring police chiefs, 'Even though some assignments can be grueling or seem to be a nuisance, it's good to have as much diverse experience under your belt as possible.'"

Hillard said that there are other ways to provide valuable experience to commanders who are "up and comers." In the absence of formal training in his department for command staff, he told commanders to always watch for opportunities that could serve as training opportunities. For example, he said that he told lieutenants and sergeants to attend police board meetings, because they involve various interests that police officials must work with. He said that he also encouraged command staff members to "pick up the telephone and call that chief in the next town and get some type of relationship and communications going with them."

Almost all of the chiefs said that they send promising officers to PERF's Senior Management Institute for Police, FBI executive training sessions, and programs of other federal, state, and local law enforcement associations. Some also send command staffers to nationally recognized programs for law enforcement professionals offered by colleges and universities. Some chiefs send officers to training academies run by nearby municipal police departments. Other chiefs said they have taken steps to facilitate their employees' access to city-funded financial aid to attend college.

In some cases, chiefs may use executive-level training for the express purpose of fixing a particular problem in a command staff member. One chief said he was sending a promising staff member to the FBI National Academy in hopes that he would acquire better personnel management skills. The chief said that he hoped to put the command staffer in a position to succeed him, but the staff member had an overly aggressive personality with subordinates, a problem that needed to be addressed.

Succession Planning

In the end, Bratton said, "the proof of the strength of an organization is in its ability to hold together when the principals depart." A chief should avoid building an organization that is so dependent upon his or her presence that it becomes as inflexible and resistant to change as a petrified tree, Bratton said. A key to succession planning is that "the first bench has the responsibility for bringing along the second bench."

Transparency and inclusion are the hallmarks of chiefs whose departments have a good chance of surviving their departure, Bratton said. As much as possible, members of a police department should know what is going on across the entire department and what the chief thinks about it. By contrast, "exclusion is a bad management strategy," Bratton said.

Succession planning involves more than grooming a future chief, Hurtt said. Rather, a chief owes the community a long-term plan for addressing the future needs of the department, he said. "When I leave my department, I should have a plan in place that I can leave for the next guy," Hurtt said. That plan should project the future needs of the department for infrastructure such as vehicles, computers, and radios, he said, and should also include plans for staffing the department.

Chapter 5

Working Well with Your Bosses, The Community, and Your Employees

It's About Relationships

There is an interesting paradox involved in being a police chief. The responsibilities of the position are enormous, beginning with the fact that policing is a life-and-death job every day. And a chief needs to bring a wide range of skills and talents to the job, in areas ranging from budgeting and personnel management to communications and politics. Yet even though the demands on a chief are great, chiefs are given surprisingly little authority to act unilaterally.

As Kunkle put it, "As a police chief, you have very little power—but you share power with many."

In his current post as chief of police in Dallas, Kunkle said, he shares power with a city manager, a "strong, charismatic" mayor, 14 council members, several news media outlets, seven different police associations, and many constituency groups. "You have to be able to navigate your way through all of this or you'll get fired," he warned. "Most of my peers don't have contracts or terms of office," said Kunkle, who himself is an at-will employee in his current position as chief, and has been in every jurisdiction that he has served over the past 25 years. "When you serve at the pleasure

---

> AS A POLICE CHIEF, YOU HAVE VERY LITTLE POWER—
> BUT YOU SHARE POWER WITH MANY.
> **-CHIEF DAVID KUNKLE**

---

of those who hire you, it almost seems that you need to get 100 percent of the votes every day," Chief Kunkle said.

Like many other chiefs, Kunkle said that there are three essential parts to the business of being a police chief: (1) forging the best possible relations with the mayor, city manager, city council members, and other "bosses" to whom you report; (2) delivering on your obligations to the community; and (3) maintaining the support of the rank and file.

Kunkle offered this advice to new police chiefs: "As chief, you have to be very attuned to these three areas. If one goes bad, you probably can survive. If two out of the three start to go south on you, you probably are in big trouble."

Lansdowne said the same thing: "You've got three entities to deal with: the community, the mayor or council, and the police officers. If you make enemies of any two of those at one time, you'll get fired." The way to avoid that? "You've got to consistently understand that your decisions affect all three groups, and try to find some balance," Lansdowne advised.

Chiefs agreed that of the three "constituencies," the community is the most important. "I certainly have tried to be responsive to bosses, but I never felt that I worked for the manager or city council; I've always felt I worked for the public," Kunkle said.

Lansdowne agreed. "Chiefs protect the interests of the police department employees," he said, "but when push comes to shove, the decision has got to be in the interest of the community first, and after that, in the interest of the department as a whole."

Working Effectively with Your Mayor or Other Bosses

On the question of police chiefs' relationships with their bosses, talking to William Bratton is a good place to start. As New York City police commissioner, Bratton had a public falling-out with Mayor Rudolph Giuliani because he was bringing crime rates down sharply and was getting news media attention for it—too much attention, in the view of the mayor.

Following is what Bratton told us about working with your bosses:

People talk about "managing from the middle"—which in policing means things like using your captains to get things done. But chiefs also have to learn to 'manage up,' and by that I mean working with the people above you. In Los Angeles, I have a mayor and a police commission I report to.

"Managing up" starts with continuous contact. In New York and now in Los Angeles, it's been my practice to have weekly meetings with my mayors. The other aspect of "managing up" is transparency, in terms of not springing any surprises on them. At your weekly meetings, you tell your mayor and city council members or whoever your bosses are, "We're working on this, we're working on that." And when you plan some event, be sure to see if the mayor or city commissioners want to be a part of it. Oftentimes they do, sometimes they don't. But either way, they're not going to be surprised by something that appears on the evening news.

Of course, you can't keep them informed of everything. There are certain things that are operational that you may not talk about, or breaking news situations where you have to be out there very quickly and you don't have time to brief them or get them into the picture. But as a rule, the keys to "managing up" are continuous contact and transparency in your dealings with your mayor or other officials.

One other thing that should be mentioned is that when you are talking to your own people in the police department, you should avoid giving any subliminal messages that are negative about the people you report to, because that will shape the way your organization will deal with them. You need to keep a tight rein on your subordinates who deal with City Hall, to make sure they are handling things the way you want them handled. The people who work for you—just because they do work for you and are loyal to you—may do what they think is best to make you look good. But that's not necessarily what you want in dealing with your elected officials.

In dealing with all three constituencies, Lansdowne said, a chief needs to make as few enemies as possible. "Remember that mediation is always available," he said. You can always find some middle ground if you're willing to do that and if you learn to listen well. If you make enemies, they're enemies for life—especially politicians. They'll never let it go; they'll wait in the wings and get you."

Lansdowne offered another cautionary note: "Never, ever, make decisions when you're angry," he said. "Don't say things when you're angry, because it'll come out, and once the press gets hold of it, you can't take it back. They'll run with it and you'll end up kicking yourself. Also, when *other* people are angry or upset about something, try to slow it down. Your people come in and tell you the mayor's upset, the council is upset. Try to wait until everyone has calmed down. Then you can have some meaningful conversation and figure out a solution together. But when people are angry or excited, it's difficult to manage through to a solution."

Deane has had an unusually long tenure as chief in Prince William County: 20 years. Asked how he managed that feat, he said, "I've stayed out of the politics of things. I've consciously avoided ever going to anything that smelled like a political event. Of course everything you do is political to some degree, but I've avoided events that are politically partisan or that support a particular candidate."

Furthermore, Deane said, "You may like one board member more than others, or have more respect for some of them than others, but I carefully try to treat them all the same."

Deane offered one more piece of advice to chiefs who would like to last more than a few years in the job: "Try to say 'yes' as often as you can." However, he added, "I've never allowed politicians to influence who I hire, who I fire, or who we arrest."

> NEVER, EVER, MAKE DECISIONS WHEN YOU'RE ANGRY.... ALSO, WHEN OTHER PEOPLE ARE ANGRY OR UPSET ABOUT SOMETHING, TRY TO SLOW IT DOWN. YOUR PEOPLE COME IN AND TELL YOU THE MAYOR'S UPSET, THE COUNCIL IS UPSET. TRY TO WAIT UNTIL EVERYONE HAS CALMED DOWN. THEN YOU CAN HAVE SOME MEANINGFUL CONVERSATION AND FIGURE OUT A SOLUTION TOGETHER.
> **–CHIEF WILLIAM LANSDOWNE**

Depending on the form of government in a particular jurisdiction, a police chief may report to a mayor, a city manager, city council members, police commissioners, and/or other officials. But the chiefs interviewed for this book generally said that the character, personality, and management style of the chief's "bosses" are at least as important as the type of governing structure in the jurisdiction. Strong, powerful mayors can be especially challenging to work with, chiefs said. And even in cities where the position of mayor, from a legal standpoint, is largely ceremonial, an aggressive mayor with a strong political power base can be a force to be reckoned with, they added.

Most chiefs interviewed for this book have worked either under the "strong mayor" or under the "city manager" form of local government. Many have worked under both systems at different points in their careers, and were able to contrast these experiences.

In a "strong mayor" system, which generally is used in big cities, including Chicago, Boston, Philadelphia, and New York, the city council has legislative authority, but the mayor has executive-branch authority over city agencies, including the police department. The police chief reports to the mayor, and the chief's fate is generally tied to the fate of the mayor, and to the mayor's support for the chief.

In a "city manager" system, used in many medium-size cities, the city council has both legislative and executive authority, and the mayor usually has less formal executive authority or may even be limited to ceremonial duties. The chief reports to a city manager—a professional government manager hired by the council. The chief must also work directly with city council members.

Mayor vs. City Manager Form of Government: The Difference Is in the Politics

Stephens said that the difference between working for a mayor as opposed to a city manager is a matter of "the politics," and most chiefs agreed with this observation. However, the chiefs had different perspectives on which form of government is more political, and how politics affects the role of the police chief.

Kunkle said he has never worked under the "strong mayor" form of government, but based on what he sees happening in other departments, he believes it is preferable for police chiefs. "The

BERNARD MELEKIAN DISCUSSES
HOW A CITY MANAGER
VIEWS THE ROLE OF POLICE CHIEF

Bernard Melekian has an interesting perspective on the relationship between a police chief and City Hall. He spent 23 years in the Santa Monica Police Department before being named chief in Pasadena, Calif. in 1996. He served as chief until early 2008, when the Pasadena city manager announced her retirement and Melekian accepted the position of Pasadena city manager on an interim basis. But Melekian made it clear that he wanted to return to the chief's job as soon as a new city manager could be found, and he returned to the chief's job in October 2008.

Asked to comment on his experience as chief and as city manager, Melekian offered this detail that may be interesting to chiefs: He said that when he was police chief, it was easier to get his phone calls returned than when he was city manager.

But the critical insight that Melekian gained from his experience as city manager was this: "What it made me realize is that the city manager *doesn't want to have to think about* the police department. The view is that the police department should take care of itself."

This is unfortunate, Melekian said. "In a lot of ways, police chiefs are disconnected from the workings of city government, even though things like city planning and zoning and economic development impact public safety and are impacted by public safety," he said. "I think we need to do a better job of involving our young police managers, our lieutenants and captains, into the city's planning processes."

Melekian gave an example of what he means: "For years we've had a problem with homeless persons going through people's trash. They clean out the recyclable bins and sell the cans and bottles. It's a neighborhood nuisance, and we were getting a ton of complaints about it. So as city manager, I sat down with the acting police chief and the public works director and got them to put together a program for a couple weeks to go out and target these scavengers. A police officer was assigned to ride along with the public works person and write citations when he saw people scavenging through the trash."

The point is that when city agencies do not work together, problems fall through the cracks and are ignored. "This trash issue was not something that, as police chief, I would have thought was the police department's job. Normally public works would not reach out to the police department, and normally the police would say, 'That's not really our problem, it's a public works problem.'"

Both police chiefs and directors of other city departments would benefit from having a broader, more cohesive view of their jobs, Melekian indicated. So for aspiring chiefs, "any experience that puts you in City Hall for a while would be a good thing," he said.

thing that a strong mayor does is give a chief a source of political support," he said. "If you are a strong mayor and you like what the chief is doing, you can provide the kind of support that can't be provided under a city-manager government." The mayor's support can be especially helpful if a chief is making organizational changes in the police department or is taking on other issues that could provoke resistance, he said.

By contrast, a city manager "is constantly counting council votes," Kunkle said, in order to make sure that government activities are in line with what the city council supports. Because city managers are hired, not elected, they usually do not have their own political base. As a result, city managers are more vulnerable to what Kunkle called "bad politics"—not being willing or able to resist even a small amount of political pressure to take an action the chief considers unwise.

Complicating the picture is the fact that under the city-manager system, the fate of the police chief is not necessarily tied to the fate of the city manager. For example, Kunkle said that one city manager who hired him as police chief was fired before Kunkle took office, "so he was gone before I started my first day of work." Darrel Stephens said he had the same experience in his first job as chief.

Watson had a different perspective. In his view, the city manager form of government is less political than the strong-mayor system, and therefore is easier for a police chief to work with, because "the mayor is first and foremost a politician, while a city manager is a professional."

Hurtt, who has held two positions as chief under a city manager and one under a strong-mayor system, offered this advice: "If you're working under a mayor, you'd better recruit support from the business community. It's hard to get a mayor to make a long-term commitment, to take the long view." Business leaders can help a chief weather a storm if support from the mayor wavers, he indicated.

Yet another complication, Hurtt said, is the effect of term limits on elected officials. Laws that limit a mayor or city council member to a certain number of terms in office "have hurt public safety" by exacerbating the instability of city government, in Hurtt's view. Today, he said, in jurisdictions where there are term limits, continuity in city government is no longer found in the elected officials, but only in the police unions and in various constituencies within the community.

TODAY, CHIEF HAROLD HURTT SAID, IN JURISDICTIONS
WHERE THERE ARE TERM LIMITS, CONTINUITY IN CITY
GOVERNMENT IS NO LONGER FOUND IN THE ELECTED
OFFICIALS, BUT ONLY IN THE POLICE UNIONS AND IN
VARIOUS CONSTITUENCIES WITHIN THE COMMUNITY.

Candidates for a chief's position should study the city's governance structure, chiefs said. If you are a candidate for chief in a city that operates under a strong mayor form of government, it is important to know how much time is left in the mayor's term, whether the mayor is planning to run for re-election, and how police chiefs and other city agency administrators traditionally have fared when new mayors take office. If you are considering a position in a city-manager form of government, you need a clear sense of the manager's views of the lines of communication between the police chief and the manager, and between the chief and the city council. "A police chief needs to keep the manager informed," Stephens said, "but it is not practical to communicate to the council through the manager on *all* issues, as some expect."

Remember Who Your Boss Is

The first principle of building a productive relationship with your boss, Esserman said, is to remember who is the boss in the relationship. He said that he will never forget a piece of sound advice that he received from Lee P. Brown, former commissioner of the New York City Police Department, public safety commissioner in Atlanta, and chief in Houston.

"If you've got a problem with your boss, *you've* got the problem, not him," Brown said.

Another thing to remember, O'Toole said, is that chiefs need to try not to upstage their mayors. And sometimes that is easier said than done, she added. "As the first female Commissioner in Boston, I was often approached by the news media for feature stories," she said. "In most instances, I declined, explaining to reporters that I had no desire to be a celebrity or a politician. It would be a lose-lose situation for me: If the story came out negative, it was bad for me; and if the story came out positive, it was bad for me. The mayor's staffers would say, 'What are you doing on the front page of the paper? It should be the mayor.' But as a woman police commissioner, the media treated me as a novelty, often writing the stories whether I cooperated or not."

Be Judicious about Politics

Finally, chiefs said that another key to building a good relationship with your bosses is to try to "stay above the fray" if the police department becomes the focus of political posturing. One chief found his future up in the air a year after he joined a department, because a candidate for mayor made replacing the chief a central element of his platform. That candidate won the election, but backed off firing the chief when the community rallied to the chief's defense.

Even though the experience was stressful, this chief spoke without rancor about it, considering it one of the calculated risks of working in a political environment. "Every mayor has a choice about who he wants to serve as police chief," the chief said. "And the news media like the controversy." The chief said that today he enjoys an excellent relationship with the mayor.

But there is an important difference between generally avoiding politics and declining to take positions on political issues that a chief *should* be involved in, chiefs said. They advised their colleagues not to duck when it is a matter of leveraging your influence to advance your mission.

"I learned that as much as possible, you try to stay out of politics," Ramsey said. "That doesn't mean you don't support causes that may end up being political, such as gun control. The secret is

> I LEARNED THAT AS MUCH AS POSSIBLE, YOU TRY TO STAY OUT OF POLITICS. THAT DOESN'T MEAN YOU DON'T SUPPORT CAUSES THAT MAY END UP BEING POLITICAL, SUCH AS GUN CONTROL. THE SECRET IS TO NEVER LET THE AGREEMENTS OR DISAGREEMENTS GET PERSONAL. BELIEVE IN THE CAUSES YOU GET INVOLVED IN, AND ARGUE THEM ON THEIR MERITS.
> –COMMISSIONER CHARLES RAMSEY

to never let the agreements or disagreements get personal. Believe in the causes you get involved in, and argue them on their merits."

In practice, chiefs said they look for a good balance between being political and being apolitical. Hillard said that his mayor told him, "You handle the department, I'll handle the politics." But in reality, Hillard said, a chief can't avoid getting caught up in the political part of that equation. "I answer to the mayor, and that's the bottom line," he said. "If things don't turn out right, you are going to get taken to the woodshed. I got taken to the woodshed a lot, but that's part of the job. I knew it wasn't personal. And the mayor did not allow anyone *else* to kick my butt."

Hegerty said that, in retrospect, she wishes that she had learned these lessons a little earlier in her tenure as chief and had been more sensitive to the intricacies of building a constructive relationship with city officials. "I had to come to terms with the reality that city council members hold the vote; I don't," she said. "The lessons that I learned are: Don't get cross-wise of the city council, and remember that it is important to them that they be able to save face. If they find themselves backed into a corner on a controversial issue, you will probably be the loser. They control the money and the staff. And they have a statute protecting their power."

At the same time, Hegerty offered advice about playing hardball with politicians when it becomes necessary. "The chief needs to defend the department and its officers when they come under unwarranted criticism from elected officials," she said. "Different venues are available to accomplish this, such as opinion editorials in the local newspaper. I took on any number of aldermen when they publicly blamed the police department for not doing enough to reduce violent crime. I found that if a chief speaks out when unwarranted criticism is leveled, it sends a message to the other

> I ANSWER TO THE MAYOR, AND THAT'S THE BOTTOM LINE. IF THINGS DON'T TURN OUT RIGHT, YOU ARE GOING TO GET TAKEN TO THE WOODSHED. I GOT TAKEN TO THE WOODSHED A LOT, BUT THAT'S PART OF THE JOB. I KNEW IT WASN'T PERSONAL. AND THE MAYOR DID NOT ALLOW ANYONE *ELSE* TO KICK MY BUTT.
>
> **–SUPERINTENDENT TERRY HILLARD**

elected officials that the chief is not afraid to strike back. It makes the elected officials more cautious in their criticism of the Police Department. It also garners the support of the department members when a chief stands up and defends them publicly."

Communicating with the Boss:
What You Tell Them and When You Tell Them

Chiefs strongly recommended making certain that your bosses are kept in the loop on any news that may have political repercussions—good or bad—for them. "Don't surprise the mayor," Esserman said. "You are the most visible, politically powerful person in the city after the mayor. But he's elected, and you're not. You are part of his team."

Another important aspect of communication is getting your bosses on board with your vision for the department. "It's your job to sell your vision to them," Ramsey said. "Not just the mayor—talk to the city council members too. If you leave a void, they'll take it. I had to tell them what I would do."

In fact, in Bratton's opinion, getting your bosses to buy into your vision for the department *before* you take the job is a key determinant in how you will fare as chief, and failing to get "buy-in" should be a deal-breaker when you are considering a job as chief. Bratton, who has worked with governors, mayors, and city commissions during his career, said that "to be successful as a chief, you have to share the vision of the person bringing you on board. And in my experience, you may go in as compatible, with a shared vision, but that can change over time. When the vision is no longer shared, you move on."

THE CHIEF NEEDS TO DEFEND THE DEPARTMENT AND ITS OFFICERS WHEN THEY COME UNDER UNWARRANTED CRITICISM FROM ELECTED OFFICIALS…. IF A CHIEF SPEAKS OUT WHEN UNWARRANTED CRITICISM IS LEVELED, IT SENDS A MESSAGE TO THE OTHER ELECTED OFFICIALS THAT THE CHIEF IS NOT AFRAID TO STRIKE BACK…. IT ALSO GARNERS THE SUPPORT OF THE DEPARTMENT MEMBERS WHEN A CHIEF STANDS UP AND DEFENDS THEM PUBLICLY.

–CHIEF NAN HEGERTY

Keeping the Lines of Communication Open

Chiefs said that while there may be a natural inclination to save communications with your bosses for the best and the worst of times, it is in the best interests of the chief and the department to find some way of keeping their bosses apprised of routine activities of the department. Olson advised chiefs to be proactive in giving their bosses periodic activity reports. "Otherwise, you do good work, and nobody knows it. Activity reports make it hard for bosses to come down on the chief for not doing anything or not keeping them informed. And if you're ever really attacked, it's all there," Olson said.

Beginning with his first chief's job, Olson said he gave his bosses two-week, monthly, and year-end reports on his "activities, actions, views, and thinking." These reports did double duty for him, he said, not only keeping city officials apprised of his activities, but also "helping me stay on course."

The nature of a chief's contacts with his or her mayor will depend on the interests and personality of the mayor, chiefs said. For example, Davis said that his mayor has an intense interest in news coverage of the city, so Davis talks to the mayor every morning "to give him my take on what is happening in the community on crime issues." Davis's public information person also meets once a week with the mayor's office, and has daily contacts with the mayor's staff.

Davis also said that he finds himself struggling to keep pace with the mayor, who spends a great deal of his time out in the community, meeting with his constituents, and expects his police chief to be out there with him. "The number of public events the mayor goes to is amazing," Davis said. "He's out in the community every

---

> DON'T SURPRISE THE MAYOR. YOU ARE THE MOST VISIBLE, POLITICALLY POWERFUL PERSON IN THE CITY AFTER THE MAYOR. BUT HE'S ELECTED, AND YOU'RE NOT. YOU ARE PART OF HIS TEAM.
> –COLONEL DEAN ESSERMAN

single day of the week. I have to work 12 to 15 hours a day just to spend an equal amount of time in and out of the department."

Flynn cautioned that the chief needs to be alert to how his or her staff gets along with the mayor or manager's senior staff. "If you're not attentive, a palace guard syndrome can set in," he warned. "You can't let a disagreement between your chief of staff or press person and the mayor's undermine your relationship and access. You can be badly undermined by people who have the mayor's trust for no more serious reason than they don't like something that somebody on your staff said, or is rumored to have said."

Chiefs also need to keep an eye on what's happening in neighboring jurisdictions' police departments, because their bosses react when something goes wrong nearby. As one suburban chief said, "If a neighboring city has a scandal, I get an audit."

Weighing in on Command Staff Appointments

Chiefs expressed different opinions about the extent to which bosses should be engaged in the selection of command staff for positions that the chief has the authority to fill. However, most chiefs said that whether or not the mayor or city manager's approval is needed to fill command staff posts, it's a good idea to keep the boss in the loop.

A number of chiefs said they discussed their preferences for command staff appointments with their mayors in advance, only to be instructed by the mayors to make their own final decisions. By contrast, another chief said that his boss asked him to keep the existing command staff in place. "This department is very parochial and the mayor was very comfortable with the existing command staff," this chief explained. "I said I would work closely with them, and if there were problems, I would come to him. That's the way it is sitting now."

Several chiefs said that they make a particular point of consulting with their bosses on any personnel actions that might produce controversy or draw news media attention. Chiefs should keep in mind that officers may have their own back-channel communications with council members, Burack noted. The news media like stories that involve controversy, so if a chief has a feeling that a personnel action might provoke a backlash, it usually will, McNeilly said.

Timoney expressed a different point of view, saying he does not discuss command staff changes with his bosses in advance. "I don't give anyone a heads up, because if you do, they will try and stop you," he said. However, Timoney said that he does provide a rationale for his decisions, and he keeps his bosses informed and tells them that they should have no problem picking up the phone and asking him what is going on.

When You and the Boss Disagree

What if the mayor's ideas conflict with those of the chief? "You have to talk to them about it, and you never go public when you and your boss disagree," Ramsey counseled. Esserman said that if he is asked to do something that he doesn't agree with, he "tries to find compromise," or if the issue does not allow for compromise, "I will try very hard to change the mayor's mind."

"In the end, you have to be willing to walk" if a mutually acceptable agreement cannot be reached, Esserman said, adding that that is why he has insisted on having a contract for every chief's job that he has held.

Getting to Know Your Community

The chiefs who were interviewed for this book agreed that new chiefs should know from the start that managing the police department is only part of their job; they also need to build strong relationships with the community. As Hanson said, "Take care of the internal, but stay connected to the community."

The underlying reason why police-community relations are so important is that public safety is a critical factor in the health of a neighborhood, chiefs said. "When people are unhappy with public safety, they vote with their feet," Hurtt said. "They move away."

Chiefs can gain considerable insight into the public safety concerns of residents by tapping into the institutional knowledge of commanders and beat cops on the street. But that is no substitute for a chief going out into the community to get a firsthand feel for the community, chiefs said.

In every encounter throughout the day, chiefs should try to appear approachable, Hurtt said. Even a 20-second conversation

> IT IS REALLY IMPORTANT TO GET A SENSE OF WHAT
> THE COMMUNITY WANTS FROM YOU. THE MORE
> LISTENING YOU DO, THE MORE YOU LEARN.
> THE MORE COMMUNITY MEETINGS YOU GO TO,
> THE MORE QUESTIONS YOU CAN ANSWER.
> **–COMMISSIONER ED DAVIS**

with a citizen during an elevator ride can help build support for a chief and his mission, he noted.

Meeting the public also helps chiefs to verify what they are being told by their troops, Ramsey said. "You have to get off your butt, get out of your office, ride the streets, go to meetings, and see for yourself what the situation really is. This helps you identify problems before they occur."

Davis said that the best piece of advice that he can give on building relationships with the community is to spend more time out of the office than in the office. "It is really important to get a sense of what the community wants from you," he said. "The more listening you do, the more you learn. The more community meetings you go to, the more questions you can answer."

The importance of listening was underscored by one chief who said he has found that new chiefs tend to make two big mistakes in their efforts to build relationships within the community: "They do all the talking during their initial contact. And then they don't go back."

Engaging the Community: How Some Are Doing It

Davis said that it is not enough for chiefs to meet with residents themselves. "There are just too many people for the chief to have a relationship with each one," he said. So in addition to having their own community meetings, chiefs must get their officers involved, he said. And that means making community policing a department-wide philosophy. "Officers should know the people on their routes," he said. "I have been spreading this message through training and constant references to the philosophy of community

[ON SHOWING RESTRAINT IN ANSWERING CRITICS]
AS MY GRANDMOTHER USED TO SAY, IF YOU STOP
TO KICK EVERY DOG THAT BARKS AT YOU, YOU'RE
NEVER GOING TO MAKE IT INTO TOWN.
-CHIEF HAROLD HURTT

policing. I am going to roll call after roll call after roll call to talk about this."

Furthermore, "just talking philosophy doesn't get it done," Davis said; the community needs to see evidence that the chief is acting on that philosophy and has asked his officers to engage the community in problem-solving. To that end, Davis has implemented a strategy to get officers into the community to meet the citizens they serve. "I am having officers go out and fill out a card for every business on their route—to meet with business owners, get contacts for who we should call at night or during the day if there is a problem. At the same time, we're giving officers' contact information out. We're getting good information, and this also gives the officers an opening to talk to the people who run the stores."

Hurtt said that when he decided that he needed to talk to more people in the community, he turned to faith-based organizations. "Reaching out to the religious community is especially important in Houston, where there's a church on every block, and every minister is king," he said.

Finally, chiefs advised their colleagues to keep in mind that working effectively with community interests is not a popularity contest. Despite their best efforts, chiefs must accept that not all of their actions will be well received by every constituency. A chief constantly makes decisions that may alienate certain sectors of the community, and must learn to live with the reality that he or she can't satisfy everyone all of the time.

Hurtt also urged chiefs to exercise restraint in responding to those who oppose their actions. "As my grandmother used to say, if you stop to kick every dog that barks at you, you're never going to make it into town," he said.

The Issue of Race Relations

Several chiefs stressed that prospective and new chiefs need to familiarize themselves with race relations in the communities that they serve. "Most cities have racial tensions," Timoney said. "The level of tension may vary from time to time, but it's always a component of the city's history."

Where there are racial tensions in a community, these chiefs said, a new chief needs to know about the situation in order to begin to address it early on—and to avoid saying or doing anything that could inadvertently make the situation worse. For example, Stephens said that in one city where he served as chief, there was some lasting sensitivity in the African-American community about a number of shootings that had taken place before he became chief, "so it was important to connect with the faith community" early in his administration.

Timoney said that he has found that even clashes between the police and racial minority groups dating back 20 years can leave an indelible mark on police-community relations. "Sometimes there are old wounds that are not easily healed, and you have to be cognizant of that," he said. "You need to know the history that impacts the present day."

Davis said that community outreach is a major component of his efforts to improve race relations between the police and citizens. First, that involves bringing groups of officers together with community groups to talk about issues of race. And a second part of his program involves "bringing community members into the police academy so they can see firsthand the kinds of training that police officers receive. "I want the community to understand the training that police receive, so they'll understand why police do what they do," he said.

> MOST CITIES HAVE RACIAL TENSIONS. THE LEVEL OF
> TENSION MAY VARY FROM TIME TO TIME, BUT IT'S
> ALWAYS A COMPONENT OF THE CITY'S HISTORY.
> **–CHIEF JOHN TIMONEY**

STEPPING UP TO RACIAL ISSUES

By William Bratton

Many political leaders are reluctant to talk about race issues, and that's understandable. Race can seem like the "third rail" of public policy issues. If you do speak out, you may find that your remarks are taken out of context by the news media, and before you know it, you're accused of being racist.

I have known for many years that for police chiefs, racial issues are particularly sensitive. As a young officer in Boston in the 1970s, during the height of the school desegregation crises there, I saw firsthand how the police can find themselves caught up in the middle of racial controversies.

This phenomenon goes back to the origins of policing in America, to the pre-Civil War era, when police agencies were expected to enforce the laws of slavery, and for a century after that, when police enforced segregation laws. This legacy has engendered among our African-American populations a real distrust and fear and in some cases outright hatred of the police.

More recently, in the 1970s and '80s and '90s, police tried to restore order in areas of our cities that were in the grip of crime and drug crises, and the unfortunate reality is that crime and disorder in our country are concentrated in poorer neighborhoods, and often the poorest neighborhoods are minority neighborhoods. And there have been times when police have been perceived to be, and in some cases have been, unnecessarily brutal as they try to suppress crime.

The point is that police agencies, by their nature, have been a flash point for racial tension, because police work involves getting into the middle of discord and strife.

However, I believe it is a mistake for police leaders to be silent on race issues and to try to avoid involvement in situations that have racial aspects. I say this because I believe that we in policing, instead of being the flash point, can be on the cutting edge of resolving racial tensions. Instead of being perceived as part of the racial problem, police can be in the forefront of a movement toward understanding and peace between racial and ethnic groups.

>> *continued on page 88*

>> *continued from page 87*

In fact, because police agencies are inherently in the thick of things, I believe that there is no type of government agency that has a greater opportunity to have a positive impact in minority communities. If we "get it right," we can not only work to ameliorate the legacy of difficult relations between police and racial minorities, we can establish ourselves as the branch of government that takes the lead in effecting positive change on racial issues.

By "getting it right," I mean finding ways to reduce the violence and fear that is so prevalent in many of our minority neighborhoods. I mean policing consistently, compassionately, and Constitutionally, and adopting the principles of community policing.

What does that mean in practice? It starts with building relationships. When I knew I was going to become chief of police in Los Angeles, even before I arrived I made a point of looking at the news media coverage of the Police Department. I asked myself, who are the people who most frequently criticize the LAPD? What are they saying? What are their issues? And I visited many of them before I took the job, to get their perspectives. A case in point is John Mack, who served as head of the Urban League in Los Angeles and for 35 years was the most prominent civil rights leader speaking out against police abuses that he felt were directed against the city's African-American population. Today, John is my boss; he's president of the Police Commission. The relationship that he and I developed helped us work together on racial problems, first when he was head of the Urban League and later when he became my boss.

Another example is Connie Rice, a very well-known civil rights attorney who has successfully sued the LAPD many times. I made a point of reaching out to Connie to try to get an understanding of what she felt were the issues that needed to be corrected in the Police Department. This led to me appointing her head of the blue-ribbon commission that recommended reforms stemming from the Rampart scandal.

You can go a long way as a police chief just by making sure you have "face time" with people—getting to know them, letting them get to know you, and learning to understand each other. It involves simple things like going out to the meetings in church basements, and talking to the African-American news media and the Latino media.

In this way, even if you end up agreeing to disagree on an issue, at least things don't devolve into the stale old rhetoric. And relatively minor issues don't become "deal-breakers," because you have built up trust in each other over time. And the more you talk to people, the more you realize that there is a lot of common ground to stand on.

In general, it is far better to work on building your relationships as soon as you can, and not to wait for a controversial incident or other crisis to erupt before you pick up the phone. It is much easier to resolve a crisis if you already have a well-established relationship with the people who are involved.

However, it is also true that a crisis can serve as an opportunity to improve your relations with minority groups. For example, following the MacArthur Park incident in 2007, where the LAPD botched the handling of an immigration rally, I worked with many Latino leaders I had not dealt with before, and in a very short period of time they helped me to understand their positions, and we developed good relationships that continue to this day.

Currently, racial issues in policing are getting compounded by the immigration issue. In fact, I believe that the immigration issue is more about race and ethnicity than it is about immigration, because many immigrants look different from a lot of the people who are complaining about them being here. Some chiefs may not share that view. But on the immigration issue, racial issues, and any other issues that are seen as "hot button" and politically dangerous, I believe it is a mistake for police chiefs to shy away. You'll do a better job, and be a better chief, if you try to capitalize on the fact that police departments by their nature are in the middle of these controversies. Use that power to reach out to all the different people in your community, especially the ones who may be criticizing you.

Keeping the Support of Your Officers and Working with Unions: Finding Common Ground

An ability to manage labor relations is critical to the success of a police chief, according to chiefs interviewed for this report. Hurtt said it bluntly: "Unions are why chiefs sometimes only last for two or three years." Stephens indicated that he was an example of union problems causing turnover in chiefs' jobs; one of the reasons he left the chief's position in one department was that he became weary of fighting with union leaders, and he was hired as chief in two jurisdictions in part to fix labor problems.

Most chiefs interviewed for this book said they have had good and bad relationships with police unions in their careers in law enforcement, depending on the circumstances of the particular agency. For example, Timoney said that in one city where he worked, there were at least five police unions, and "all of them were pretty decent; they kind of knew there was a line you don't cross." But in another department where he served as chief, "there was a God-awful union that fought everything; it literally was a daily battle."

The chiefs interviewed for this report agreed that a controversial labor-management dispute can undermine a chief's ability to lead by disrupting police personnel, creating problems for the chief's bosses, and causing fear in the community. In a worst-case scenario, a labor dispute can overshadow all of the positive aspects of a chief's tenure, and even force the chief's resignation or dismissal. Mayors and city council members sometimes will force out a chief in order to get a labor dispute out of the headlines, chiefs said.

> [ON THE IMPORTANCE OF
> MOTIVATING YOUR EMPLOYEES]
> YOU HAVE TO FOCUS ON THE PEOPLE. WHEN A CHIEF
> LEAVES A DEPARTMENT, THE PROCESSES HE OR SHE
> HAS PUT IN PLACE CAN BE ABANDONED OR REVERSED.
> BUT NOBODY CAN CHANGE THE PEOPLE THAT YOU
> MENTORED. THEY CAN'T CHANGE THEIR MOTIVATION,
> DRIVE, VALUES, AND SKILL SETS.
> –CHIEF MICHAEL BERKOW

Most chiefs said that the problems that they have encountered with unions centered on their relationship with union leaders, not with the rank and file. These conflicts generally arise when there is disagreement between the chief and the union leaders over what is in the best interests of the officers and the department. When union leaders are pursuing actions that are well-grounded in the concerns and needs of their constituents, there is a good chance that the chief and the union will be able to resolve the dispute. In the chiefs' view, the trouble arises when union leaders have agendas that are not in the best interest of their members, and may not even reflect officers' feelings about the issues in dispute.

When a chief and a union leader reach an impasse, chiefs said that having good relationships with their officers and strong political bases in their communities improves their chances of prevailing.

Get Your Officers Behind You

Kunkle described his strategy for reducing conflict with police unions: "Keep the lines of communication open with your officers. Deal directly with the rank and file. Walk around and talk to officers. Listen to their grievances."

Other chiefs agreed with this strategy. Among their comments: "Treat your officers with respect and as professionals.... Be as transparent with and accessible to your own officers as you are with other department stakeholders.... Communicate effectively with them. Let them know what you are doing, and why you are doing it. Give them an opportunity to have input on actions that will have a direct effect on them.... When you deviate from department policy, explain your rationale for doing so. And when there is a disciplinary problem with an officer, keep your command staff in the loop. They are the direct link with your officers. And if they understand and support your actions, there is a better chance that your officers will understand as well."

Berkow said the importance of treating officers well came to him as an "epiphany" that shaped his thinking about how a chief can really be a change agent. "What I realized," Chief Berkow said, "is that you have to focus on the people. When a chief leaves a department, the processes he or she has put in place can be abandoned or reversed. But nobody can change the people that you mentored. They can't change their motivation, drive, values, and skill sets."

CHIEF CHARLIE DEANE TALKS ABOUT THE IMMIGRATION ISSUE AND ITS IMPACT ON OFFICERS

There are few issues in policing as controversial as the extent to which local police agencies should be involved in enforcing federal immigration laws. And with the possible exception of Maricopa County, Arizona, nowhere has that issue flared up hotter than in Prince William County, Va.

Among his peers (as well as newspaper editorial boards and large segments of the public), Chief Charlie Deane has won acclaim for the skill with which he has handled the immigration issue, which caused tremendous upheavals across his county in 2007-08. Faced with a Board of County Supervisors that seemed determined to crack down hard on illegal immigrants, Deane managed to successfully convince the lawmakers to avoid the most extreme measures. He spoke out forcefully, warning that an overly strict policy could cause severe damage to the Police Department's community policing efforts, could spur vigilantism and divide the community, and could cause the county to be viewed as a racist community. He also educated the board about the financial costs of the various proposals they were considering. At the same time, he took on a strong public profile in letting the public know about how the measures would affect them.

Deane's skill in working with two of his constituencies on the immigration issue—the Board of Supervisors and the community—has been thoroughly documented and is a story that is widely known. But there has been little focus on how he worked to ensure that his third constituency—Prince William police officers—would stick with him as the department moved forward in enforcing a new law that the Board of Supervisors approved, increasing the role of the police in immigration enforcement.

"I worried about the officers probably as much as anything, because I didn't want to lose their confidence," Deane said. "This was such a new issue, and even though I have always had a good relationship with my officers and I talk to them as much as I can, I didn't have a strong feeling as to where the majority of them were on this issue. I was concerned that some of them might feel I was trying to constrain them, to hold them back from getting into overly aggressive immigration enforcement, because I was making public statements about how we needed to be cautious about it, about how complex the issue is legally, about all of the costs of it."

"But I communicated with them internally as frequently as I could, and I made sure that all of my command staff was involved in developing the policies [to implement the law]," Deane said.

"As it turned out, I think the officers were with me all the way. I think the fact that I was getting beaten up on the issue by some members of the public and some board members caused the officers to rally around me. It also helped that I made sure that the Board of Supervisors put some money into the budget for this. So the officers knew that I understood that there was work involved in this, and that if the board wanted to do this, they had to provide us with more positions to do it."

O'Toole said that sometimes the chief's role is to serve as a middleman between police unions and the mayor's office or other city officials. "It can be tricky," she said. "I had to walk a tightrope between maintaining strong lines of communication with the unions and not giving city hall any reason to think that I was disloyal or selling out to the unions. When I first walked in the door as commissioner [in Boston], the city and the unions were in the middle of a nasty contract battle that had been going on for some time. Even though the contract was usually negotiated between city hall and the unions, I offered to step into the middle and try to encourage a resolution of it. I found that often it was more difficult negotiating with the city officials than with the union negotiators, because city hall staffers were taking such a hard line. The point is, as police chief, you sometimes end up playing referee. I often said to both sides, 'There are enough people on the outside shooting at all of us without us shooting at each other.'"

Communication skills are the key to establishing good relations with union leaders, O'Toole said. "We had four unions," she said. "I met with all of them immediately and said, 'I don't care what time of day or night you call me. If you have an issue, I'd rather know about it from you face-to-face than read about it in the *Boston Globe* or the *Herald*. I won't play any games if you don't play any games.' It really worked. We successfully resolved many conflicts. There were times when we disagreed, but I can honestly say the union leaders were fair and never made it personal with me."

Davis said that chiefs should try to maintain a good relationship with union leaders as long as they can. "There will always be things that you can work with them on," he said. "But once there are non-negotiable items out there, you need to enlist help from other people. You cannot take on a union leader head-to-head and win. You need to get your side of the story out there, and you have to be strategic about it. You need to have a political structure behind you, and you need others to get your story out."

Reach Out, Stay Close . . . But Not Too Close

Even when chiefs have had bad experiences with unions, they should try to reach out to them, out of respect to the officers whom they represent, Timoney said. Stephens said that a new chief should begin by doing some homework. "Read the union contract; take a look at recent grievances and arbitration issues," he said. "Make an early contact with union officials, and talk with them about your respective roles and how to go about building a good working relationship with them."

"Stay as close as you can to the unions," was the advice of Hegerty, who enjoyed a productive relationship with the head of Milwaukee's police union. She and the union leader talked on a regular basis, she said. "There were some things that we didn't agree on, but we had a very professional relationship and tried to resolve things informally as much as possible."

On the other hand, some chiefs said they have been careful to let union leaders know they are not interested in getting *too* close to the unions. "I told the union guy, 'I didn't come here looking for a bride; I'm already married,'" one chief said.

Timoney said that even as he reached out to the union in one city, he told the leaders, "I am here to run the department, and I am not looking for assistance or to share my managerial responsibilities. But I'll back you up on pay issues."

There can be a lot of variation in the particular union situations in different cities, Kunkle indicated, and sometimes things get complicated. He said that infighting among the four police unions in his city has diverted their attention away from the department leadership to some extent. "These guys challenge each other as much as they challenge management," he said. "It makes it hard to communicate with them, because each one believes that the others are getting something at their expense."

Aim for a Cordial, Respectful Relationship

Chiefs advised their colleagues to aspire to cordiality, respect, and fairness in their relationship with unions. The goal should be to find common ground when there is a disagreement. Chiefs should remember that the art of negotiation usually involves searching for a solution that gives both sides something they can call a "win." And when there is no common ground, the parties should agree to disagree and leave the negotiating table as professionals.

Surviving a No-Confidence Vote

Union votes of "no confidence" in police chiefs have become increasingly common, but some believe that the more often this tactic is used, the less effective it becomes. All of the chiefs interviewed for this report who experienced no-confidence votes survived the experience. One chief survived no-confidence votes in two communities. McNeilly held his position for an additional eight years after a no-confidence vote against him. Davis held a position for six years after 80 percent of the officers voted in favor of a no-confidence statement. Hurtt said that an attempt to secure a no-confidence vote against him failed when "the union lost the PR battle."

Perhaps the public has grown weary of no-confidence votes that seem trivial. In Chief Kerlikowske's case, the no-confidence vote "was over a written reprimand of one officer," he said.

This is not to say that a no-confidence vote is painless. "When I first heard about it, it was like a kick in the gut," McNeilly said—even though he knew that the vote did not reflect the views of many of his officers. The source of the no-confidence vote was a "rabble-rouser" who had a history of problems with the department and was being investigated. "A lot of people in the department knew this guy for what he was, and some came to me to say they had become so disillusioned with the union that they didn't go to union meetings anymore," he said.

Chiefs also should keep in mind that when a union holds a no-confidence vote, it does damage to itself, McNeilly said, because it is shutting itself off from the police chief and hurting any chance for resolution of other pending issues—which is something the union members understand.

Chapter 6

Transparency and Accessibility: The Hallmarks of an Effective Media Relations Strategy

Managing the War of Words

Chiefs interviewed for this book agree that an important part of a police chief's job is establishing effective relationships with members of the news media. "The days of responding 'no comment' to media inquiries are long gone," said Hillard. "If you don't have a relationship with the news media, you're going to lose this war of words. If you have a good relationship with the press, you'll get a good bang for the buck, and they will treat you fairly and squarely."

Chiefs were of one mind on the importance of media relations. Following is a summary of what they believe: *News media stories have a significant influence on how the people to whom chiefs are accountable—their mayors and other "bosses" and the public—view the performance of the police. Some chiefs may need to fight a natural inclination to avoid contact with the media. They should be guided by the reality that if the news media don't get information from the police, they will get information elsewhere, often from biased and poorly informed sources. And when that happens, chiefs find that they are responding to media inquiries from a defensive posture.*

Chiefs advised their peers to be transparent and accessible to media representatives. Transparency means being honest and open about both good and bad news in the police department. Accessibility means having mechanisms in place to ensure that reporters can get answers to their questions in a timely way.

Davis said that he has found that some departments do not have a tradition of transparency and accessibility. The Boston Police Department traditionally "played it very close to the vest," he said, and in his initial meetings with command staff, he found that "the biggest problem they identified was the leaks in the Police Department. There was almost an unhealthy obsession with it. I told the command staff, 'I'm not going to have any problem with leaks, because I am going to tell the media pretty much everything.' That didn't go over well. But I have made a commitment to bringing transparency to the department."

Maintaining an open-door policy toward the news media can help ensure that reporters will be in a position to learn the good news about the department and its activities. Bratton said the message that he communicates to his commanders and officers about media relations is, "Give me a good story to tell, and I will tell it. Give me something else, and unfortunately, I will have to tell it like it is."

"I recommend giving the news media accessibility, transparency, and a degree of wariness," Bratton added. "They are not your friends in a professional way. The nature of their business is to tell a story, and oftentimes, they think that uncovering something bad is a better story than telling the story of some success. And while you might have friendly personal relationships with reporters, when you put your professional hats on, they have their obligations and we have ours. I don't think I've ever resented them. I try to understand them, and in understanding them I try to influence them, but at the same time I understand that I don't control them. I've always recognized that it's much better to try to work with them than working against them."

I WISH THE MEDIA WERE DIFFERENT....
I WISH I THOUGHT THAT THEY CARED ABOUT TRULY
PROVIDING BALANCED STORIES. I DON'T THINK THEY
DO. BUT IT DOESN'T MATTER WHAT I THINK ABOUT
THEM. THEY ARE A FACT OF LIFE FOR ANY POLICE
CHIEF, AND TO TRY TO IGNORE THEM OR THINK
YOU'RE GOING TO WORK AROUND THEM CAN BE A
FATAL MISTAKE.

–CHIEF BERNARD MELEKIAN

Timoney advised his colleagues to try to understand the nature of the job of reporters. A chief who has frequent contacts with reporters will come to understand what reporters need to get their jobs done.

For example, McNeilly said that any time there was an officer-involved shooting in his department, "the majority of my command staff came out, and the media knew they were going to have a comment before they went home."

Frequent interactions with reporters will also help a chief to learn which reporters are fair and thorough, and what kind of stories they like. That kind of understanding can help chiefs recognize a positive story about the police department when they see one, and to know which reporters are most likely to do a good job writing the story. "Give them opportunities to publicize positive stories about your department," Timoney said. For example, Timoney opened Compstat meetings to the press, knowing that the liveliness of the meetings would appeal to reporters and would generate stories about the effectiveness of Compstat in fighting crime.

Police chiefs need to work with the news media even if they find themselves disappointed in how the news business operates, Melekian said. "I wish the media were different," he said. "I've always tried to be very open, transparent, forthcoming on issues. And my strategy is to return every call, to answer every question, and if there's some reason why I can't answer a question, to explain why. But I wish they were more responsible. I wish I thought that they cared about truly providing balanced stories. I don't think they do. But it doesn't matter what I think about them. They are a fact of life for any police chief, and to try to ignore them or think you're going to work around them can be a fatal mistake."

When the News Is Bad

Chiefs should not pull back from their interactions with the media when the coverage turns negative. "They are going to write the story with or without you, so it is important that you step out front with the story," Ramsey said. "Don't hide anything," Myers said. "Get out in front of issues that may be of interest to the media while things are still calm and controllable." For example, Myers said that when he learned about an officer who was a pedophile, he immediately held a press conference about it, which he said

> DON'T HIDE ANYTHING [WHEN THERE IS BAD NEWS].
> GET OUT IN FRONT OF ISSUES THAT MAY BE OF
> INTEREST TO THE MEDIA WHILE THINGS ARE STILL
> CALM AND CONTROLLABLE.
> **–CHIEF RICK MYERS**

galvanized community support for the department's handling of the situation and, he believes, helped to manage the media attention that it received. The incident was "on the news for only one day," he said.

Cultivating the Media

The key to working effectively with the media is "to develop a relationship with some individuals in the media whom you trust, who you feel are fair," Cline said. "Then, whenever you have the opportunity, you cultivate them."

Cline said he began learning this lesson when he was a sergeant working in narcotics, and a reporter wrote an article asserting that the police were doing nothing about drugs on the street. Cline called the reporter when a major narcotics operation was about to go down, and invited her to see what the police in fact were doing about the narcotics problem. "We got a positive front-page article about the operation," he said.

Looking after media relations can be a time-consuming process, Esserman said, because "you need to keep educating and reeducating the press as reporters come and go."

Several chiefs said that they schedule regular meetings with reporters and editors. Hurtt has a "media availability"—an open meeting with reporters in which the chief does not necessarily make an announcement of a news development, but simply takes reporters' questions—on a monthly basis, and he meets with the *Houston Chronicle* newspaper editorial board on critical issues. "This has worked for me," he said.

Kerlikowske, who also meets frequently with news media editorial boards, said he uses these opportunities to discuss issues that potentially could draw media attention. And holding general meetings with the media can save time, because "that way

NEW TECHNOLOGIES GIVE CHIEFS MORE OPTIONS FOR TAKING THEIR MESSAGES DIRECTLY TO THE COMMUNITY

A number of chiefs, in particular Darrel Stephens, pointed out that having an effective news media operation should be only one aspect of a police chief's strategy for getting a police department's messages out to the public. In recent years, the Internet and other technologies have opened up many new methods of police-community communications—and the communicating can go in both directions, Stephens noted.

In Stephens' home of Charlotte-Mecklenburg, for example, as in many other cities, the Police Department Web site allows anyone with access to a computer to obtain many kinds of information: crime statistics, crime maps for their neighborhood or any other particular location, news about particular crimes or other developments, crime prevention tips, links to victim services and other resources, information on Most Wanted persons, and so on. Also available are the department's official policies and procedures on dozens of issues, from use of force to police employee sick leave policy, as well as selected local ordinances. A section on the Police Department's services "From A to Z" provides separate pages on dozens of topics, from Accident Reports to Youth Services. A variety of video programs also are available on the Web site, in which police employees explain various aspects of police operations.

Residents also can use the Charlotte-Mecklenburg Police Department's Web site to report a crime, to sign up to automatically obtain e-mail alerts about crime or neighborhood events, to file an accident report, to file a complaint (or commend an officer), or to send an e-mail to the Police Department in order to ask a question.

Charlotte-Mecklenburg's Web site provides instantaneous access to Police Department information in ways that would have been almost unimaginable a generation ago. And in cities like Los Angeles, police department Web sites are so extensive that one could easily spend days navigating them and studying all of the information that is available.

Ed Davis noted that the Boston Police Department has begun a blog on its website that offers constant updates on crime

>> continued on page 102

>> continued from page 101

statistics, investigations, arrests, and other information. The blog and the Web site "get thousands of hits a day," including many from the news media, he said. "A lot of the reporters are downloading the information that we are writing and putting it in articles," he said. The department has a person assigned to overseeing the blog on a full-time basis.

In San Diego, Bill Lansdowne said he has obtained excellent community feedback regarding the new types of information-sharing provided by technology. "We have these 'information blasts' where we send crime information to all the community groups, and they love that," he said. "If there's a series of burglaries in a neighborhood, we'll send out the information over the Internet, and the community groups distribute it to all their members, and they're happy to get it. They say it's more than they see in the press, and they get it first, before the press."

Charlie Deane said that his department's Web site has been a valuable resource in helping to counter false information regarding the illegal immigration debate, which has been extremely contentious in Prince William County, Va. A number of local advocacy groups established blogs on the issue, and "unfortunately, some of these blogs are a lower form of communication than a grocery-store tabloid," Deane said. "With some of them, there's no attribution to anything in them, so people just say things that aren't true. They anonymously attack the police and make false statements, and yet people take it as gospel."

Deane said that his department's Web site was useful in responding to the attacks and bringing a measure of reasonableness to the debate. "I was able to put documents on our Web site such as my verbatim presentations to the Board of County Supervisors," he said. "That way, we could put out there what I wanted to say, exactly the way I wanted to say it, rather than how someone else might say I said it. And sometimes that's important not only to get your message out at the time, but also as something that people can refer to later. We can say, 'I publicly said such and such, and it's been on our Web site for six months, and that's a fact.'"

However, chiefs should not delude themselves that they can use the Internet and other technologies to take their messages directly to the public and thus avoid the need to deal with traditional news media, Bernard Melekian of Pasadena, Calif. cautioned. "I recently read a survey that we commissioned in our city about where people got their information," he said. "And the city's Web site, and by extension the police department's Web site, is still a relatively small number, about 15, 18 percent. You still have about 35 percent of the people who say they get their information from newspapers, and probably more than that from TV."

"So I think the new communications technologies are great," Melekian said, "but the newspaper is still going to generate people's interest and form the initial impression. If an incident occurs, most people are going to learn about it when they see it on TV or in a newspaper headline. They may then choose to do their own research, but if they do what most people do, they Google it, and what does that produce most of the time? Other news media sources. So you can't choose to not deal with the media and say, 'I don't need reporters; I'm going to deal directly with the community.'"

I don't have to deal with every reporter on every issue," he said. Kerlikowske also said he makes it a point to compliment reporters when they write a good story. And he is not reticent with editors "if a story is grossly unfair."

Flynn strongly recommends that chiefs write an occasional opinion piece for the editorial page of the local "paper of record." He noted, "If you've been accessible, and done the editorial board thing, you'll find the editors are open to giving you an opportunity for extended commentary on an issue, policy, or strategy. In an era of 'sound bite' journalism, this is a rare opportunity to communicate, unedited, to your community and to your cops. You get to go on the record on your terms."

Staffing the Media Relations Function

Most chiefs interviewed for this book said they have someone on their staff assigned to handle media relations. Several chiefs said that the first thing they did upon taking over the top job in their departments was beef up their media relations staff.

In Seattle, Kerlikowske built up the Police Department's capacity to respond to media inquiries, and media relations personnel are on duty from 7 a.m. to 10 p.m. during the week, and on call on weekends. Kerlikowske said he meets with department media relations officers on any sensitive issue in order to ensure that the messages issued by the department are consistent, and he encourages department media officers to "find good stories" to release to reporters.

If resources permit, chiefs said, hire someone who is trained in media relations. And if you have a media relations person, let that person do his or her job, chiefs said. In small agencies, the chief may handle media relations without assistance from a media

---

YOU'VE GOT TO BE ACCESSIBLE AND VERY OPEN. WHEN I WAS CHIEF IN PITTSBURGH, SOME REPORTERS HAD MY HOME PHONE, AND A FEW THAT I KNEW WELL HAD MY PERSONAL PHONE NUMBER. I WOULDN'T DO THAT FOR EVERYONE, BUT I FELT COMFORTABLE WITH A FEW REPORTERS THAT I TRUSTED.

–CHIEF BOB MCNEILLY

officer, and the task is probably easier than handling the press in a big city, in Burack's view. "I think it's easier," he said. "The reporters are people I see at the grocery store. You just have to approach it in terms of cultivating the relationship, being open with them, and getting information for them."

The Chief Must Be Accessible

Most chiefs agreed that having a media relations staff does not alter the importance of the chief being accessible to the press. "I just think that for a chief, it's part of doing business that you have to talk to the press," Esserman said.

How accessible should a chief be? "You've got to be accessible and very open," McNeilly said. "When I was chief in Pittsburgh, some reporters had my home phone, and a few that I knew well had my personal phone number. I wouldn't do that for everyone, but I felt comfortable with a few reporters that I trusted."

Timoney said that although he has a public information officer, "almost every reporter in town has my phone number." Asked how he can manage that level of media accessibility, he laughed and said, "It's pretty easy. I don't have much of a life."

Davis has a different system. He has not given the press his phone number; they all go through his public information person. However, over the course of a day, the PI person makes a list of reporters who have called and who need to be called back. "Toward the end of the day, I do a series of press calls, and she is on the phone with me," Davis said.

Bratton said that being accessible at serious crime scenes and other major events is an important element of his media relations strategy. "Not to command or control," he explained, "but to be there."

> [ON FINDING TIME TO TALK TO REPORTERS]
> ALMOST EVERY REPORTER IN TOWN HAS MY
> PHONE NUMBER. [LAUGHING] IT'S PRETTY EASY.
> I DON'T HAVE MUCH OF A LIFE.
> **–CHIEF JOHN TIMONEY**

FBI PUBLIC AFFAIRS CHIEF JOHN MILLER, FORMERLY AN AWARD-WINNING REPORTER, OFFERS ADVICE ON MEDIA RELATIONS

John Miller has been on both sides of the fence. In his current position at the FBI and a previous stint at the New York City Police Department, he has served as the chief spokesman for law enforcement agencies. He also held a top post at the Los Angeles Police Department, in charge of counter-terrorism and major crimes bureaus.

And he has had a stellar career in journalism, at ABC News and other organizations, winning nine Emmys and many other awards. One of his many achievements was a 1998 interview with Osama bin Laden.

At PERF's 2008 annual meeting, Mr. Miller offered police chiefs the following advice about how to approach news media relations in the 21st Century:

The first thing you need to know about reporters is they are not your friends. The second thing you need to know is they are not your enemy. In large measure, they are what you make of them. Don't look at every encounter you have with a journalist as a jousting match. Try to see it more as a civics lesson. You're the professor, teaching reporters about what the police are doing, why they are doing it, how they see their role in the community, and so on.

If you're getting crummy coverage, 50 percent of it may be that the media are just giving you lousy coverage, but 50 percent may be because you're failing in this ongoing civics lesson.

Get your good news out fast, and get your bad news out faster. That sounds easy enough, but having had jobs in the news business as well as policing, I know it can be difficult, because sometimes it takes a while even for the police to get to the bottom of things.

I remember that when I was a reporter and there was a big police story, the official story from the police department was sometimes a long time coming. So I never sat around waiting for the official story. I ran around talking to witnesses, the victims, to officers, and anyone else who might have something to contribute to the story. And as I was doing all this, I'd be trying to piece it all together, testing what one person said against what others said.

In 1994 I took the public information officer job at the New York Police Department, and a week later there was a police shooting incident. Now, I thought, this should be a lot easier. I had full access to everyone and everything. I could cross the yellow tape. I could interview the officer involved, even as he was undergoing emergency room treatment. I could talk to everyone at the police command center.

So I'm stringing all the information together about the shooting. *And I'm finding that none of it fits at all.* In fact, as time went on, from the first hour to the second hour to the second-and-a-half hour, the story kept getting blurrier and blurrier. I was driving *backwards* on the information highway.

So I turned to John Timoney and said, "For the love of Jesus, I've been doing this for 20 years, and now I'm on the inside— where I always thought you were huddled together with all the information right in front of you. But I'm finding we don't know **** here!"

And Chief Timoney, looking at me like I'm a pathetic child, says, "Oh, Johnnie me boy, let me explain to you the first lesson of policing: If there's trouble getting the information, it's usually because there's trouble with the information."

This would become my mantra.

Police chiefs also need to understand that the news business is moving much faster than it ever has before. It's not like you wait for the morning paper and then the 6 o'clock news and then the 11 o'clock news. There's all-news-all-the-time on cable, on the Web, on radio. There *is* no news cycle, because the cycle doesn't stop.

So you have to be more agile, more adept, and more careful. When something big happens, don't make the mistake of waiting until you're certain you have a 100-percent accurate version of the entire story before you say anything to the media. Somewhere in the first hour, somebody should say something. If you don't become the source, if you don't say, "I'm going to take control of the information here and become the go-to person," you'll soon find yourself trying to catch up to what has become a runaway story. Remember, the media are on all the time, which means if they don't have you on air, they will find somebody else. And you talk about so-called experts. On some of the cable stations, it seems that you qualify as a terrorism expert if you directed traffic in Mayberry for 10 minutes and got thrown off the force.

So when something big happens and you're still trying to get all the information, go out and say something, and start off with this: "The information I'm about to give you is preliminary. It is likely that it will change. Let us tell you what we know. Let us tell you what we don't know. And let us tell you when we're going to come back to update this."

Share the Limelight

Despite his prowess in dealing with reporters, Bratton said he makes a point of sharing news media attention with his staff. "My style is not to be the face of the department all of the time," he explained. "I don't need to give every press conference or be quoted in every article."

Likewise, Timoney said that he encourages his command staff members "to get themselves on TV and in the newspapers. Some of them hate the press, but most are pretty comfortable talking to reporters, particularly when they get the OK from above. And for the most part, they have performed well."

Ramsey said that when the news is bad, he handles media contacts himself, and when the news is good, he lets his media person make the call. He sometimes asks a commander or patrol officer to talk to a reporter, if that is what the reporter wants.

Hegerty said that a key focus of her media strategy was to build media confidence in her officers. "The media trusted me, but not always the officers," she said. To remedy the situation, she worked on "putting the officers out front" by giving all department personnel training in media relations.

The importance of media training for police personnel was echoed by several other chiefs. Their comments indicated that, while not long ago media training might have been restricted to top command staff, more departments in recent years have been making this training available to sworn personnel with the rank of sergeant and above.

McNeilly said he became a strong proponent of media relations training for his command staff after taking a course himself. Esserman said he does not provide media training for staff, but only because "I never ran into training that I liked." Instead, he said, "I give them guidance. If they make mistakes, I correct them in private."

CHIEF CHARLES RAMSEY SAID THAT WHEN THE NEWS IS BAD, HE HANDLES MEDIA CONTACTS HIMSELF, AND WHEN THE NEWS IS GOOD, HE LETS HIS MEDIA PERSON MAKE THE CALL. HE SOMETIMES ASKS A COMMANDER OR PATROL OFFICER TO TALK TO A REPORTER, IF THAT IS WHAT THE REPORTER WANTS.

Looking for Fair Coverage

Building a good relationship with the media "is everything," and a poor relationship with the media is second only to inadequate funding among factors that can undermine a chief's ability to do his or her job, Kerlikowske said. And what counts, most chiefs indicated, is whether the coverage is fair. The biggest challenge in media relations, in Hegerty's view, is that reporters cover bad news but often seem uninterested in good news.

In general, however, McNeilly said he believes that "the media does a good job trying to get things out there fairly and presenting both sides. For the most part, we've gotten a fair job from them."

Chapter 7

Succeeding as a Woman in Policing: Putting the Gender Issue in Perspective

There is no doubt that women have advanced in the field of policing over the last few decades. The most recent study by the Bureau of Justice Statistics (BJS) found that as of 2003, 11.3 percent of the full-time sworn personnel in local police departments were women, up from 10.6 percent in 2000 and 7.6 percent in 1987. Women are most likely to be found in the largest police departments. In departments serving populations of one million or more, 17.3 percent of the officers were women, according to the BJS study. (That figure declines steadily as the size of the population served declines, to a low of 5.7 percent female officers for departments serving fewer than 2,500 residents.)

Furthermore, a number of national, international, and state and regional associations have been formed to serve the interests of women in law enforcement, including the National Center for Women and Policing (NCWP), Women in Federal Law Enforcement (WIFLE), and the National Association of Women Law Enforcement Executives (NAWLEE). According to the latter group, recent counts indicate that approximately 300 women serve as chief executive officers in municipal, county, state, and federal agencies. Promotional opportunities for those women are expanding, according to NAWLEE President Patty Jaye Garrett Patterson, chief of police in Sumter, S.C. And according to Chief Patterson, the vast majority of female policing executives "are willing to reach out to other women who aspire to achieve and excel." NAWLEE is designed to serve as a venue for that kind of encouragement, networking, and sharing of knowledge, she said in a recent letter to NAWLEE members.

> I DO KNOW THAT THERE IS STILL SOME RESISTANCE
> BY MEN, ESPECIALLY TO HAVING A FEMALE AS THEIR
> LEADER, BUT IT IS NOT AS OVERT AS IT ONCE WAS.
> I'M NOT BLIND TO THAT FACT, BUT WHAT I TRY TO DO
> IS FOCUS ON THE POSITIVE ASPECTS THAT WILL ALLOW
> ME TO BE SUCCESSFUL IN MY JOB.
> **–CHIEF ELLA BULLY-CUMMINGS**

Today, many police agencies actively recruit female officers, and have pages on their Web sites devoted to debunking myths about women in policing, explaining the application process, and encouraging women to seek a career in policing.

Still, the research is thin on issues pertaining to women in policing, and in particular the challenges faced by women police chiefs. Because four of the chiefs interviewed for this report are women, and all of them are ground-breakers, we seized the opportunity to ask them about their careers and the paths they took to reach the highest positions in their agencies. Ella-Bully Cummings was the first woman to be named chief of police in Detroit. Ellen Hanson was the first woman officer hired in Lenexa, Kan. and one of the six founders of NAWLEE. Nanette Hegerty was the first female chief in Milwaukee. And Kathleen O'Toole was the first female commissioner of the Boston Police Department.

The chiefs generally rejected the notion that the challenges that they faced as they advanced in their careers differed significantly from those of their male counterparts. "I don't believe that there are unique issues for women in policing," Hegerty said emphatically. She acknowledged that three decades ago when she entered policing, she encountered male colleagues who did not think that women belonged on a police force. However, she said that by and large, she found that people were "vastly supportive" of her and that she was accepted by police professionals and elected officials without regard to her gender. Thus, she recommended that aspiring chiefs who are female "shouldn't waste their time worrying about their gender."

In fact, the female chiefs said they believe that their unwillingness to make an issue of their gender has been a key factor in their male colleagues' acceptance of them. Don't make a big deal about being a woman, they advised their peers, and it will be less likely to become a big deal. Calling attention to your gender, the chiefs said, will only make your job more difficult.

Bully-Cummings said that she "didn't think about the female thing" when she was asked to become chief in Detroit, where she has spent her entire law enforcement career. Since then, she has tried not to call attention to her status as a woman in policing—"because I've had so much work to do." (Focusing on her work has been a lifelong pattern with Chief Bully-Cummings; she put herself through college and law school even as she advanced through the ranks of the police department.)

That is not to say that Bully-Cummings did not experience sexism. When she joined the Detroit Police Department in 1977, some male officers would call in sick rather than work with her on a patrol shift. "It was the initial impact [of bringing women onto police forces] that was difficult, taking people out of their comfort zones," she said. "So some male officers would either call in sick or go home sick. But that has changed. Today I don't think that in the city of Detroit there is any conflict between men and women working in a squad car together and supporting one another and backing one another up. I do know that there is still some resistance by men, especially to having a female as their leader, but it is not as overt as it once was. I'm not blind to that fact, but what I try to do is focus on the positive aspects that will allow me to be successful in my job."

In the end, succeeding in policing, Hanson said, "is not so much about the battles that women have to fight because they are women. The real key for women is to work hard, hold on to your principles, and not allow being a woman to become 'baggage' that you carry with you onto the job."

Pitfalls and Lookouts

While they downplayed the impact that being female had on their careers, the chiefs said there are challenges that are unique to women who pursue law enforcement careers. All of these four women, each of whom has spent 30 or more years in law enforcement, described "pitfalls and lookouts" that women in policing should be aware of as they make their way in a field that still is largely the province of men.

Hanson cautioned that "the women who succeed in policing are the ones who have learned not to try too hard to become one of the boys." Female police officers "have to learn very early on how you perceive yourself personally and where you fit in. You have to hold on to a significant degree of your femininity. You don't want to be so rough and ready that you put off your male colleagues. On the other hand, you don't want to come across as prissy."

At the same time, Hanson said that women police officers will find that they are "not going to have a peer group," so it is more critical for women than men that "you be comfortable with yourself and have a good sense of yourself."

This observation was echoed by Bully-Cummings, who said that a four-year break from policing early in her law enforcement career, when she was laid off due to a budget crisis, halted what she believes in retrospect was a youthful attraction to the "macho cop" culture. "That layoff saved me," she asserted. When she returned to law enforcement, she had matured and was no longer interested in the perception that law enforcement is a strong or "masculine" field. Instead, "I was all about the business, and everyone knew it," she said.

Hanson, who rose through the ranks to become chief of the department where she started her career, suggested that coming to the position of chief from inside the department may be easier for a woman than coming from the outside. While there are no national data available on that subject, it is interesting to note that all of the women interviewed for this book became chief of the department where they began their careers.

O'Toole said she feels fortunate not to have experienced a great deal of sexism in her career. "I have lots of female friends in policing who have spoken of horrendous experiences," she said. "They've been harassed, they've been discriminated against. I've been blessed because I've worked with some great mentors, like Bill Bratton, who just made it clear that he would not tolerate that nonsense. And when I worked in [Massachusetts Gov. William] Weld's Cabinet [as Secretary of Public Safety], seven out of his 11 Cabinet Secretaries were women, so that was another environment where women were obviously valued. I've had some issues over the years, but more so with individuals, not with systemic sexism or discrimination."

For O'Toole, advancing in a police career, for a male or a female officer, is a matter of establishing credibility, and that begins early

> IN POLICING, WE ALL HAVE TO ESTABLISH OUR
> CREDIBILITY. IT STARTS WHEN YOU'RE IN THE FIELD
> AS YOUNG POLICE OFFICERS AND YOUR LIVES DEPEND
> ON EACH OTHER.... COPS RESPECT PEOPLE WHO HAVE
> BEEN IN THEIR SHOES. BY THE TIME YOU'VE RISEN
> THROUGH THE RANKS, YOU EITHER HAVE A GOOD
> REPUTATION OR YOU DON'T.
> **–CHIEF INSPECTOR KATHLEEN O'TOOLE**

in one's career. "In policing, we all have to establish our credibility. It starts when you're in the field as young police officers and your lives depend on each other," she said. "I'd like to think that any positive reputation I established was earned when I was working out in the field as a beat cop or decoy officer. Cops respect people who have been in their shoes. By the time you've risen through the ranks, you either have a good reputation or you don't."

O'Toole said that one of the most difficult aspects of being a female police commissioner was that it brought her more attention than she wanted. "I was the first female commissioner in Boston, so it was a real novelty. I got a lot more exposure than I wanted," she said. "There were some great 'puff pieces' written about me that I wasn't looking for. It always created more hassle than it was worth. I can remember one day in particular. There was a wonderful nine-year-old boy who had a rare disease and the Boston Police had adopted him as one of our own. He marched in parades, rode on police horses, and attended many of our special events. Our hockey team did some events to raise some money to help his family. So one day I went down to the large HQ conference room to present a check to his parents. It was just an internal event and I was told there were no media there. But somebody snapped a picture of me and this little boy in his Boston Police uniform. I had my arm around him and we were looking at each other adoringly. To my surprise, the picture was splashed on the front page of the local tabloid, the Boston Herald, the next day. When I walked into City Hall that morning, it was clear that the mayor's media spokesman and chief of staff were not at all happy with me."

OBSERVATIONS FROM
GROUNDBREAKER ELLEN HANSON

Ellen Hanson has 33 years of experience in law enforcement and 17 as chief in Lenexa, Kansas, a department with 90 sworn and 46 civilian employees. She was one of the founders of the National Association of Women Law Enforcement Executives. When asked why relatively few women are rising to leadership positions in policing, she agreed with her colleagues that the most pressing issue is a decline in the pool of qualified women who might one day be tapped to become chief. "I think fewer capable women are entering policing now," she said, "and others are not staying because they don't like the police job."

But there is another problem, she noted. Female police officers face the same quandary as women in other fields: the conflict between family life and the demands of the job. And in policing, where top positions are considered a "24-7" job, the problem is especially acute. "If a woman has a family, it is a self-selecting process," Hanson explained: A female officer with children may not feel able to take advantage when an opportunity for advancement presents itself. So the officer waits, and "by the time the family is grown, the opportunity has passed you by."

Hanson also asserted that the law enforcement profession overvalues physical ability as a core competency in policing, and suggested that physical demands may be too large a factor in supervisors' decisions about promoting women or men to the more difficult jobs in policing. "We still don't do a very good job getting women into the tough jobs where they can prove themselves," she said. "The careers of women in policing have to be managed carefully, so they don't default to assignments like the DARE program officer," she explained. "The whole issue of success for women in policing is competency—and being where people can see your competence."

Hanson believes that there is a need for a shift in police values, with less focus on physical abilities and a harder look at "what makes a good leader."

Hanson added that women who succeed in policing need to do a better job of mentoring female officers, and leveraging their own experiences to help women under their supervision to advance in their careers. "We are going to have to reach down and plant the seed, delivering the message that policing is a great opportunity for women," she said.

At the same time, women who are interested in advancing in policing should not be shy; they should ask to be mentored and show a strong interest in moving up, Hanson said. Hanson described a situation in which a female officer came to her saying that she felt ready for promotion to sergeant, and asking why she had not been encouraged to take the sergeant's exam. Hanson said she told the officer, "Because I was waiting for you to *ask*." While the lack of opportunities for advancement continues to be the main reason that women are not rising to leadership positions, some female officers' reticence about pursuing opportunities also is a contributing factor, she said.

Finally, women should be proactive in preparing for and pursuing career advancement, Hanson said. "Pick a successful man *or* woman that you admire," she said. "Look at who you are, what kind of traits you display, and compare them to the traits of the person you admire. And then try to capitalize on your own strengths while incorporating the best traits of those you respect."

Status of Women in Policing

Reflecting on the progress of women in policing, the chiefs lamented what they see as a decline in the number of women entering the field. Women tend to be detailed-oriented and conscientious workers, and because of those characteristics they make good leaders, chiefs said. But there are only a relative handful of women chiefs, and with fewer women entering the field today, the outlook for an increase in women in law enforcement leadership positions may be disappointing.

According to O'Toole, even where steps have been taken to facilitate women's entry into law enforcement, there still are too few women candidates. When requested, the Massachusetts Civil Service Commission created a special certification for female police officer candidates to increase the numbers, O'Toole said. This provided women with a more even playing field, helping to balance the state's absolute veterans' preference and other considerations that have favored male candidates for entry-level positions. O'Toole said that despite the special certification, she found herself quickly exhausting the pool of qualified women candidates. "We need to do a better job recruiting women to policing in the United States," she said. When O'Toole left Boston and took a top policing job in Ireland, she found an entirely different situation. "The last recruit class in the Irish national police was 42 percent female," she said.

Chapter 8

Conclusion: Different Measures of Success

Summaries of What the Chiefs Said

On the overall responsibilities of chiefs . . .

Police chiefs have different ways of describing their job. "Policing today is a business, and the chief's job is CEO," said Harold Hurtt. In that capacity, a chief must be a politically savvy leader, an effective communicator, a good listener, an aggressive crime fighter, an able and sophisticated administrator, an adroit negotiator, and an expert at balancing various responsibilities.

Others had a more philosophical approach to describing the job, saying that succeeding as a police chief means standing for something and doing the right thing. It is about having a vision and maintaining a focus to realize that vision.

On the qualifications for the top job . . .

A number of chiefs agreed that the defining qualification for the job of police chief is a love of policing and a passion for the job. Many chiefs also agreed that a strong sense of integrity and honesty is a critical requirement. Empathy and a sincere interest in other people were often mentioned, as well as a temperament for exercising restraint in the use of the power and authority that come with the job. Of course, they said, a strong work ethic is a must.

Chiefs also spoke of finding a good "fit" with a department—large vs. small; urban vs. suburban or rural; smooth-running vs. troubled—that will complement the chief's experience and style of leadership. Personal issues also figure in whether a particular chief's job is right for you—in particular, whether you and your family will be content in the community that you will be serving as chief.

On transitioning to chief . . .

Once you take a new job as chief, the experienced chiefs interviewed for this book urge you to "trust, but verify" as you get to know your new department. It is important to listen to what people tell you, but you also have to "get in there and get a feel for the situation yourself," as one chief put it. Take as much time as you reasonably can to get to know the skills and capabilities of your senior staff before you make decisions about the makeup of that staff, experienced chiefs advised. Even if you have the opportunity to make wholesale changes in an inherited command staff, it's usually a mistake to do so, some said.

On advancing your mission . . .

Be tough, confident, and decisive in your role as a change agent, and get moving on your plans for change early in your administration, when the department and the community are *expecting* changes to happen, chiefs said. Incoming chiefs have a limited window of opportunity to make changes relatively easily, so they should strike fast in the first year or so to implement reforms, some said. "Forget about enjoying a long honeymoon," as one chief said. But be thoughtful about the department's history, and weigh the risks in making changes.

On police officer misconduct . . .

Experienced chiefs urge their colleagues to "get out in front" when it appears that a police officer may have violated a law. Call a press conference to say, "We are going to investigate this, and if the officer was wrong, we are going to admit that he was wrong." Two little words—"We're sorry"—can go far in a community that has been harmed by the inappropriate actions of police officers. "When you mess up, you 'fess up, and clean up," one chief said. And make sure that the clean-up is a comprehensive process, so that you can be confident that the mistake won't happen again.

On working with your mayor and other "bosses" . . .

Chiefs offered many suggestions about how to maintain good relations with mayors, city council members, city managers, and other officials to whom they report. Keep your bosses informed as much as possible about police department operations, and try to include them in your press conferences or other events. Spend time meeting with, telephoning, and e-mailing your bosses. Make sure that your own employees, in acting out of loyalty to you, do not inadvertently create enemies at City Hall. Avoid events that seem overtly political. Be sensitive about "upstaging" your bosses in the news media. Remember the adage that "If you've got a problem with your boss, *you've* got the problem, not him."

At the same time, however, a number of chiefs noted that when there is a conflict on core issues involving matters of integrity or the best interests of the police department and the community, chiefs must assert themselves—and even know how to play "hardball" with politicians if necessary.

On developing strong relationships with your community . . .

There are many different ways that chiefs stay connected to their communities. Go to community meetings; one chief recommended spending more time out of the office than in the office. Tap into the knowledge of your commanders and beat cops, but remember that that is no substitute for finding out yourself what is on residents' minds. Try to appear "approachable" in public; even brief encounters with community members can help build support for your goals. Reach out to community leaders. And one chief recommended exercising restraint in responding to your critics in the community.

On working with police unions . . .

Several chiefs emphasized that the key to reducing conflict with police unions is keeping the lines of communication open with union leaders. Let union leaders know they can call you at any time, chiefs agreed. Don't play games with union leaders; put your cards on the table and ask them to do the same. And stay in touch with the rank and file. Talk to officers, and listen to their grievances.

On working with the news media . . .

Building a good relationship with the media is an important part of a chief's job, the chiefs said. A poor relationship with the media is one of the top factors that can undermine a chief's ability to do his or her job. "Get to know them, but don't expect them to be your friends," one chief added. "They have their job to do, and you have yours. Try to understand the nature of their jobs."

On staying ahead of the curve . . .

A number of chiefs cautioned that it is easy to get caught up in the daily crises of police work, and forget to make time for the more substantive work that can result in long-term, lasting changes in a department. "Be proactive, and avoid finding yourself in a reactive position because you allowed an issue to spiral out of control," as one chief put it. "You can't surf behind a wave. Once you start reacting to issues, you will soon find yourself overwhelmed."

On staying focused and fit . . .

Chiefs reported having different ways of coping with the stresses of running a police department. Several said that regular exercise helps; others mentioned vacationing out of town, where they are not recognized on the street. More than one chief said that going out on patrol was relaxing. A common thread was that keeping focused and fit on the job involved "compartmentalizing"—finding a way to balance and separate the job from other aspects of your life.

How the Chiefs Measure Their Success

In the time it took to write this book, some of the chiefs who contributed to it have retired, while others are continuing their service as chiefs or have taken new positions running new police departments. One thing they have in common is that they would like to be known as "change agents" who brought improvements to the departments and communities that they served.

For many chiefs, the work for which they most hope to be remembered is their efforts to improve the quality and performance of personnel, and to build leaders within their departments and the community. As Harold Hurtt said, the responsibility of the chief "is to create an environment for others to succeed." Chiefs are aware that whether their successes are maintained after they retire depends largely on whether they leave behind a cadre of police leaders who share their vision of effective policing.

"It took me a while to come to terms with the fact that my successors all need to make their own imprints, and that it's not the programs you leave behind that truly matter, it's the quality and expectations of the people you've developed," Flynn said.

"What I get the most satisfaction from is seeing young supervisors grow into leadership positions," David Kunkle said. Dean Esserman said, "I hope that the people who have worked for me will remember me as someone who developed leaders and helped to shape how they think about their jobs."

Other chiefs said that they are most proud of their accomplishments in working with citizens and community leaders to build safer and more economically viable communities. Phil Cline said he simply hopes that his tenure as chief will be remembered as a period during which "we were successful in reducing violent crime in the city"—as well as for his role in building a police memorial to remember officers killed in the line of duty, and taking care of the families of police officers killed or catastrophically injured in the line of duty. Ed Davis had only recently begun in the top job in Boston when he was interviewed for this book, but he said he would like to be remembered for his work linking community policing and economic development in Lowell, Mass., where he served as chief for more than a decade. "Providing police services to prevent crime, especially in small business districts, is really crucial to the economic vitality and survival of the local economy," he said.

All of the chiefs would like to be remembered for leaving their departments in better condition than they found them. Chuck Ramsey was running the Metropolitan Police Department in Washington, D.C. when we asked him what he wished to be remembered for when he left the job, and he responded: "bringing credibility and respect back to the department." He recently began a major new challenge running the department in Philadelphia. John Timoney is another chief who has worked in several departments—New York City, Philadelphia, Miami—and hopes he will be known as "someone who went into tough situations and was able to turn them around, not just addressing crime problems, but improving the departments and changing the police culture in the departments."

Kathy O'Toole said that in her view, the biggest challenge faced by police chiefs is striking a good balance between crisis management and strategic management. Crises cannot be ignored, but it is strategic management that will produce long-lasting changes that improve people's lives.

"It's so easy to get bogged down in the day-to-day crises and day-to-day news media coverage " she said, "but you really need to make the time to step aside and focus on the future. Even as you deal with the pressing problems, you have to sit down and figure out how to do things strategically. You can't blame the politicians for reacting to the crises, because they have to go out there and get reelected. But a lot of people govern according to what's in the newspaper every morning, without any long-term strategic view of things. I think the police chief needs to understand that yes, you've got to deal with the crisis of the day, but you're not going to really make a difference in the long haul unless you focus on crime prevention, intervention and more efficient use of your resources."

Ella Bully-Cummings suggested that chiefs should understand that they may be having a greater impact than they realize from day to day. "When you go into a police agency that requires significant change, it doesn't occur overnight," she said. "It occurs in very small steps. In my early days as chief, I felt frustrated that even though we were doing so much, it didn't feel as though we had accomplished anything."

What changed things for Bully-Cummings was a consultant's report on the Detroit Police Department that had been completed shortly before she took office, identifying problems with the department. "I was reading the report and making notations in the margins of changes that had been effected under my tenure," she said. "And it wasn't until I did that—sitting down with a document that listed some of the problems that had been observed—that I realized that we *were* having an impact. But a police agency is like a big freighter in the water. It's very difficult to turn it around, and it's done very incrementally. Even today, sometimes my command staff will tell me that we have made some significant changes. I don't always feel that way. When you're in the forest, all you can see is the trees."

On a more personal level, chiefs said that they would like to be remembered as "good cops." They would like to leave their professional careers with the respect of those they served and they hope to be remembered for being men and women of integrity.

Finally, Bob Olson said that it's not what others think of you that is most important; what matters most is how you feel about what you have done. "As long as you are comfortable inside and feel that you did a good job, that—and family—are what count," he said.

In Bill Bratton's view, being a police chief is ultimately about improving people's lives. "Because there is often a high turnover rate for the job of police chief, people talk about 'surviving' in the job," he said. "But I think that's wrong. The job is not about survival; it's about accomplishment. And to accomplish anything in the job, you need what I call 'realistic optimism.' You need to *know* that you can achieve good results. At the same time, you need to work with reality—what are your resources, what is your current environment? If you're not confident that ultimately you're going to be able to work through the issues and derive satisfaction from working them successfully, you send the wrong message. If you get to the point where it looks like you've been backed into a corner and you're fighting for your job, it's hard to overcome the negativism of that.

"I have confidence in myself, and in the people I surround myself with, and in the profession of policing," Bratton said. "One of the things that has guided me over the years is that I know that cops count, cops matter. More than so many other components of our society, we can have a meaningful impact on people's lives, and we can do it more quickly than in most other professions."

"It's a tough business; it's not for everybody," Lansdowne said. "You've got to want it, and I think people need to understand that being chief is a real commitment. It's not an 8-to-5 job; you've got to expect that your people will be calling you all night long, all weekend long."

But even after 42 years in policing, Lansdowne shows real enthusiasm for the job. "For R and R, I'll put on a uniform, grab a marked car, and patrol the city," he said. "I do it often enough that the officers aren't surprised to see me, and community members wave. I like doing that. I feel like a policeman again. I stop on calls, get waved over by citizens, listen to people yell at me—it's great stuff!"

Biographies of the Chiefs

A Profile of the Chiefs

The chiefs who were interviewed for this book have a number of things in common—beginning with the fact that they have all contributed to the Police Executive Research Forum in many ways. Many have served on PERF's Board of Directors, and many have received PERF's Leadership Award and/or Gary Hayes Award. Many also have participated in PERF's Senior Management Institute for Police (SMIP).

The men and women quoted in this book also have vast experience in municipal law enforcement. The law enforcement careers of nearly all have spanned more than 25 years, and half began their policing careers more than 35 years ago.

These chiefs also have extensive experience in the top job. Half have spent more than 40 percent of their careers in policing as chiefs, and many have spent 50, 60, or even 70 percent of their careers as chiefs. Approximately half of the sitting and former chiefs interviewed have served as chief in two or more municipal police departments, and about one-third have served as chief in three or more departments.

Chiefs interviewed for this book are a well-educated group. The majority hold master's degrees, and several have law degrees. Most pursued their higher education as they rose through the ranks in policing. The majority have continued their education by taking advantage of professional development opportunities both within and outside the law enforcement field. Among the leadership and executive development resources that chiefs say they have found most valuable, in addition to SMIP, are the Federal Bureau of Investigation's National Academy, National Executive Institute, and Law Enforcement Executive Development Seminar; and fellowships at the John F. Kennedy School of Government at Harvard and with the U. S. Department of Justice, National Institute of Justice.

Following are brief biographies of the police chiefs interviewed for this book:

William J. Bratton is a unique PERF member. He is a recipient of PERF's Gary Hayes Award and Leadership Award and a two-time President of PERF. He was one of the first chiefs to attend PERF's Senior Management Institute for Police, and has said that SMIP was one of the defining experiences of his career. Currently, Bratton is the 54th chief of the Los Angeles Police Department, having been appointed to that position in October 2002 and reappointed to a second five-year term in June 2007. He is the former Police Commissioner of the New York City Police Department (1994–1996) and the Boston Police Department (1993–1994), and he also has held the top positions in the New York City Transit Police, the Massachusetts Bay Transportation Authority Police, and the Massachusetts Metropolitan District Commission Police. He is a U.S. Army Vietnam veteran. Bratton's critically acclaimed autobiography, *Turnaround: How America's Top Cop Reversed the Crime Epidemic,* was published in 1998. Chief Bratton holds a Bachelor of Science degree in Law Enforcement from the University of Massachusetts and was a senior executive fellow at the John F. Kennedy School of Government at Harvard University. His name has become synonymous with Compstat, a strategy for using accurate, up-to-date information about crime to devise countermeasures and hold officers accountable, which resulted in record improvements in crime rates and has become a national model. Bratton's many honors include the Schroeder Brothers Medal, the Boston Police Department's highest award for valor. Bratton first served as president of PERF during his term as New York City police commissioner and again as chief of police in Los Angeles.

Jim Burack has been the police chief in Milliken, Colo. since 2001. After graduating from Dartmouth College, he served as a police officer with the Westminster, Colo. Police Department, and later earned a law degree from the University of Colorado. He served on active duty with the U.S. Marine Corps as a judge advocate, and he was a Special Assistant U.S. Attorney for the Southern District of California. He is a lieutenant colonel in the Marine Corps Reserve, currently assigned as a liaison officer to FEMA. With PERF, he worked on the planning staff of the United Nations International Police Task Force in Bosnia in 1996. As a Marine he led a civil affairs unit in the NATO peacekeeping mission in Kosovo in 1999, and in 2004–05 he served as the Civil Affairs officer in charge of judicial engagement and reform for Anbar Province, Iraq. He holds a master's degree in criminal justice from the University of Colorado-Denver, and he is a graduate of PERF's Senior Management Institute for Police and the FBI National Academy. Chief Burack also has a special relationship with PERF, having been counsel and chief of staff to PERF Executive Director Chuck Wexler for six years. He is coauthor of *Command Performance: Career Guide for Police Executives,* one of the most popular books ever published by PERF.

Michael Berkow is the chief of police for the City of Savannah, Ga. His more than 30 years of law enforcement experience include service as deputy chief of police in Los Angeles, where his responsibilities included the Critical Incident Investigation Division, which investigates all officer-involved shootings and serious use of force incidents. Before his service in Los Angeles, Berkow was chief of police in Irvine, South Pasadena, and Coachella, Calif. Chief Berkow began his policing career in Rochester, N.Y. He also has served as a project manager with the U.S. Department of Justice International Criminal Investigative Training Assistance Program, where he managed police training and development projects around the world, including in Somalia and Haiti. This work included building police academies and establishing training programs in order to foster democratic principles of policing. In Haiti, Berkow was tasked with creating the first civilian police force in the nation's history. Chief Berkow holds a Master of Science degree in Leadership and Management from Johns Hopkins University and a Juris Doctorate from Syracuse University School of Law. He is also a graduate of the FBI National Academy and Law Institute.

Ella Bully-Cummings retired in 2008 as chief of police of Detroit. Chief Bully-Cummings was named chief in 2003, and was the first female chief in Detroit. She began her policing career in the Detroit Police Department in 1977, and rose through the ranks from a beat cop to sergeant, lieutenant, inspector, and commander, even as she obtained a bachelor's degree in public administration and then a law degree *cum laude* from the Detroit College of Law at Michigan State University. Between 1999 and 2002 she left the Police Department in order to practice law full-time. She returned to the force in 2002 and was appointed the first female assistant chief. Chief Bully-Cummings served on the board of directors of the Police Executive Research Forum, and is a member of the National Bar Association, the Wolverine Bar Association, the State Bar of Michigan, the National Organization of Black Law Enforcement Executives, and other professional organizations.

Philip J. Cline completed a 37-year career with the Chicago Police Department in 2007, retiring as Superintendent, the department's highest position, which he had held since 2003. His first beat was in the troubled Cabrini-Green housing projects, and he quickly rose through the ranks. He was promoted to detective only two years after becoming a patrol officer. He later was promoted to sergeant, and as a member of a federal Drug Enforcement Administration task force, he led a series of successful narcotics investigations. As lieutenant, Cline headed a Violent Crimes Unit. He later was promoted to Commander of Area 5 Detectives and Commander of the Narcotics and Gang Investigations Section. Later, as Chief of Detectives, he reorganized the Detectives Division and focused on reducing homicides and other crime. As Superintendent, Cline achieved significant decreases in violent crime in Chicago, with 600 fewer homicides during his three-and-one-half years as chief than in the same time span before he took office.

Edward F. Davis III has been the Police Commissioner of the Boston Police Department since December 2006. Prior to his appointment, Commissioner Davis served as the Superintendent of Police in Lowell, Massachusetts for 12 years. He began his career as a patrol officer in Lowell in 1978 and rose through the ranks before becoming Superintendent in 1994. He is the recipient of numerous awards, including the PERF Leadership Award (2002). Commissioner Davis also has served on the PERF board of directors. He holds a Bachelor of Science degree in Criminal Justice from New Hampshire College and a Master's degree in Criminal Justice from Anna Maria College.

Chief Charlie T. Deane has been a member of the Prince William County Police Department since its inception in July 1970. He served 12 years as a criminal investigator and rose through the ranks to deputy police chief in 1985, and to police chief in 1988.

Chief Deane was a Virginia State Police trooper from 1966 until 1970. He is a graduate of George Mason University with a Master of Public Administration degree. In addition, he has a Bachelor of Science degree in Administration of Justice from American University. He is a graduate of the FBI National Academy, the University of Virginia Senior Executive Institute, and the FBI National Executive Institute. Chief Deane is a past president of the Virginia Association of Chiefs of Police (VACP). He is also a member of the Policy Center Advisory Board, and a past member of the Executive Committee for the International Association of Chiefs of Police. He serves as Vice President of PERF. Among the many awards that Chief Deane has received are the Prince William County Manager of the Year, CALEA's Egon Bittner Award, and George Mason University's Wayne F. Anderson Alumni Award for Distinguished Public Service.

Dean M. Esserman, has spent virtually his entire adult life in public service as a law enforcement practitioner. Colonel Esserman served as an assistant district attorney in Brooklyn, New York from 1983 to 1987. He then served as general counsel to Chief William Bratton of the New York City Transit Police from 1987 to 1991. Esserman was assistant chief of police in New Haven, Connecticut from 1991 to 1993, where he put into effect a community-policing plan, the state's first federally funded drug gang task force, and cut crime citywide. He then became chief of police for the M.T.A. Metro North Police Department, headquartered in New York City. He served as chief from 1993 to 1998. Esserman was appointed in 1998 chief of police in Stamford, Connecticut, where he brought his philosophy of community oriented policing. Esserman is a graduate of Dartmouth College (B.A.), and New York University School of Law (J.D.), and holds a faculty appointment at the Yale University Child Study Center. He is a member of the New York and Massachusetts Bar. He is currently serving as the Senior Law Enforcement Executive-in-Residence at the Roger Williams University Justice System Training and Research Institute. He serves as a member of the board of the Vera Institute of Justice. He received PERF's Gary P. Hayes Award in 1993 and has served as a PERF board member. Colonel Esserman was appointed chief of police of the City of Providence in 2003 and presently serves in that capacity.

Edward Flynn has been the Chief of Police for the city of Milwaukee since January 2008. He began his career in the Jersey City Police Department, where he was promoted through the ranks. He served as chief of police in Braintree, Mass., and subsequently Chelsea, Mass. He later served for five years as chief of police in Arlington, Va., where he was instrumental in the recovery effort at the Pentagon on September 11, 2001. In 2003 Flynn was named Secretary of Public Safety in Massachusetts, where he was responsible for a wide range of public safety agencies, including the Massachusetts State Police, the Massachusetts Emergency Management Agency, and the Department of Correction, and where he served as Gov. Mitt Romney's chief homeland security advisor. He served as police commissioner in Springfield, Mass. from 2006 to 2008. Flynn has a bachelor's degree in history from LaSalle University, a master's degree in criminal justice from John Jay College of Criminal Justice, and has completed all course work in the Ph.D. program in criminal justice from the City University in New York. He is a graduate of the FBI National Academy and the National Executive Institute. He serves on PERF's Board of Directors and is a recipient of PERF's Gary Hayes Memorial Award.

Ellen Hanson has more than 33 years of experience with the Lenexa, Kan. Police Department. Lenexa is a city of 45,000 in the Kansas City, Mo. metropolitan area, and the Police Department has 90 sworn and 46 civilian employees. Hanson was hired in 1975 as the first woman police officer in Lenexa, and she was named police chief in 1991. She currently serves on IACP's Executive Committee and the Patrol and Tactical Committee, and is a board member and chairman of the Kansas City Metropolitan Major Case Squad. Chief Hanson was one of the six founders of the National Association of Women Law Enforcement Executives. She also has served as a member of the PERF board of directors, and is a recipient of PERF's highest honor, the Leadership Award.

Nannette Hegerty retired in 2007 as police chief in Milwaukee, Wis. She joined the Milwaukee Police Department in 1976 as one of six women in her class, and served in various assignments, including patrol, criminal investigations, vice-related investigations, and sensitive crimes. She also served as deputy director of the Training Bureau and commanded the Fifth Police District and the Juvenile Division. In 1994 President Clinton appointed her U.S. Marshal for the Eastern District of Wisconsin, a position she held until 2002. Under her leadership, the Eastern District of Wisconsin was awarded the 2001 "District of the Year" award by the U.S. Marshals Service. Hegerty was sworn in as Milwaukee's 17th chief of police, and the city's first female chief, in 2003. She was known for taking a strong stand on employee discipline following a racially charged incident in which a group of off-duty officers beat a man. Chief Hegerty fired nine officers and suspended three others, and later successfully advocated the establishment of an Employee Intervention Program. She also pushed the Fire and Police Commission for changes in the officer hiring process, including the addition of psychological investigations of recruits and a more significant role for the chief in making final decisions about hiring. Chief Hegerty holds a Bachelor of Science Degree from the University of Wisconsin-Oshkosh and a Master of Science Degree in Management from Cardinal Stritch University. She is also a graduate of the FBI National Academy as well as the FBI National Executive Institute and Northwestern University's School of Police Staff and Command. In 2004 she received an honorary Doctor of Laws degree from Marian College of Fond du Lac.

Terry G. Hillard served as Superintendent of the Chicago Police Department from 1998 to 2003. He joined the department in 1968, after serving 13 months as a Marine in Vietnam and receiving four medals and a Presidential Unit Citation. In 1975 he was seriously wounded after being shot twice while apprehending a suspect who had shot four suburban police officers. Hillard holds a bachelor's degree and a master's degree in corrections from Chicago State University, and attended PERF's Senior Management Institute for Police. After retiring from the Chicago Police Department, Hillard joined with Arnette F. Heintz, a former U.S. Secret Service official, to form Hillard Heintz, LLC, a security consulting firm. Hillard is a recipient of PERF's highest honor, the Leadership Award.

Harold Hurtt has served as the Chief of Police in Houston since 2004. He began his policing career in Phoenix in 1968 following military service. Through the 1970s and 1980s he rose through the ranks to the position of assistant chief, while earning a bachelor's degree from Arizona State University and a master's in organizational management from the University of Phoenix. In 1992 he became chief of police in Oxnard, Calif., and over the next six years he forced down crime rates while devoting attention to "equity of police service" to Hispanic residents, who make up two-thirds of the city's population. In 1998 he returned to Phoenix as chief, and focused on a high rate of police shootings. He established a video simulation training program and in 2003 made Phoenix the first major city to issue Conducted Energy Devices to all its street officers. Police shootings dropped dramatically. In 2004 Hurtt was recruited to take the top police job in Houston, and the *Houston Chronicle* noted that "perhaps Hurtt's best recommendation is the desire of Phoenix's citizenry and police force for him to stay." In Houston Chief Hurtt is known for improving police-community relations as well as reducing conflicts between police management and labor unions, and for implementing reforms regarding use of force and officer safety.

R. Gil Kerlikowske was appointed chief of police in Seattle in 2000 and served until 2009, when President Barack Obama chose him to serve as director of the White House Office of National Drug Control Policy. He began his law enforcement career with the St. Petersburg, Fla. Police Department in 1972, where he served as commanding officer of several divisions, including narcotics, criminal investigation, and internal affairs. He later served as chief of police in two Florida cities, Fort Pierce and Port St. Lucie, and was police commissioner in Buffalo, N.Y. from 1994 to 1998. He then served for two years in the U.S. Justice Department as deputy director of the Office of Community Oriented Policing Services, before returning to local policing as chief in Seattle. He has received many awards, including PERF's Gary Hayes Memorial Award in 1990 and PERF's Leadership Award in 2006. He recently was nominated for a Seattle Post-Intelligencer award for his leadership in preventing youth crime and violence. Chief Kerlikowske has served as president of PERF as well as president of the Major Cities Chiefs. He holds bachelor's and master's degrees in criminal justice from the University of South Florida, was chosen for a National Institute of Justice fellowship, and is a graduate of the FBI National Executive Institute and PERF's Senior Management Institute for Police.

David Kunkle is the chief of police in Dallas. He began his career in law enforcement in 1972 as a Dallas patrol officer. After earning his bachelor's degree in criminal justice from the

University of Texas-Arlington in 1976, he became the youngest captain in Dallas police history. In 1982 he was named chief of police in Grand Prairie, Texas, and in 1985, chief in Arlington, Texas, where he quickly made several changes, including adopting a community policing philosophy, establishing a bachelor's degree requirement for new officers without prior law enforcement experience, and implementing a workforce diversity campaign. In 1999 Kunkle joined the Arlington city manager's office as deputy city manager, where his responsibilities included the police and fire departments and other agencies. In 2004, he returned to Dallas as chief of police, and has received praise for turning around a troubled department and impacting crime in a city known for high crime rates. One of his major initiatives was to establish a Compstat program in Dallas. Kunkle, one of the first police leaders to attend PERF's Senior Management Institute for Police, is known as a hands-on police chief. In Arlington, a newspaper editor said that any neighborhood that suffered a spate of crime or gang graffiti became Chief Kunkle's new place to go jogging, the better to get a "street's-eye view" of crime. "Next thing you know he'd worked out some new version of police coverage or a new twist on community policing and the problem was fixed," the editor said.

William Lansdowne has served as chief of police in San Diego since 2003. He began his law enforcement career in 1966, when he joined the San Jose Police Department. He rose through the ranks to the position of assistant chief, also serving as a member of the California National Guard for six years. In 1994, he left San Jose to become chief of police in Richmond, Calif., where he reorganized the department and placed a new emphasis on community policing, violence reduction, and truancy programs. Homicides declined by 50 percent during Chief Lansdowne's five years in Richmond. In 1998, Lansdowne returned to San Jose to take the position of police chief, and he continued to emphasize community involvement and opening the police department to public scrutiny. He was named chief in San Diego five years later. Chief Lansdowne is a graduate of the FBI National Academy, FBI National Executive Institute, and FBI Law Enforcement Executive Development Seminar. He currently serves on the PERF Board of Directors, and has served on many other law enforcement boards and commissions.

Robert (Bob) W. McNeilly, Jr. served as chief of the Pittsburgh Bureau of Police for a decade and is presently serving as chief of police in Elizabeth Township, Pa. He began his career in law enforcement in 1977 as a patrol officer in Pittsburgh, rose through the ranks, and in 1996 was named chief of police in Pittsburgh—one week after a federal civil rights lawsuit was filed alleging that the Pittsburgh police routinely abused their powers. Chief McNeilly quickly announced plans for a series of major reforms to be carried out over five years. When the city entered into a consent decree in 1997 to settle the lawsuit, McNeilly accelerated the reform measures, which included an early intervention system that allows police managers to quickly identify potential "problem officers" while also recognizing the most effective officers. The early intervention system, new use-of-force policies, stronger training programs, and other measures implemented by Chief McNeilly have won nationwide recognition as best practices. The sweeping changes, and Chief McNeilly's reputation for being a strict disciplinarian, provoked some opposition within the department, but McNeilly enjoyed strong support across the community for taking necessary steps to solve the problems identified in the Justice Department lawsuit. Perhaps the best evidence of McNeilly's strength is the fact that he was retained as chief for a decade—more than double the average tenure for big-city chiefs. The consent decree was lifted in 2002, and today Chief McNeilly's tenure in Pittsburgh is considered a prime example of strong leadership in difficult circumstances.

Chief McNeilly has attended PERF's Senior Management Institute for Police, has served as a PERF board member, and received PERF's Leadership Award in 2003.

Bernard K. Melekian was police chief in Pasadena, California almost continuously from 1996 until 2009. (In 2008, he agreed to serve temporarily as Pasadena city manager until a new manager could be found.) In 2009, he was chosen to head the U.S. Justice Department's Office of Community Oriented Policing Services. Before taking the chief's position in Pasadena, Melekian served with the Santa Monica Police Department for 23 years, where he was awarded the Medal of Valor in 1978 and the Medal of Courage in 1980.

Chief Melekian served on the PERF board of directors from 2002 until 2006. He has served as a senior advisor for the Police Assessment Resource Center in Los Angeles, a nonprofit organization that aims to strengthen police oversight to advance effective, respectful, and publicly accountable policing. He served as chair of the California Attorney General's Blue Ribbon Committee on SWAT Policy, and was selected by Los Angeles Chief of Police William Bratton to serve on a panel to assess SWAT operations with the LAPD. Chief Melekian is a national spokesperson on issues affecting the mentally ill, and has been the recipient of numerous leadership and service awards, including the Anne B. Kennedy Award from the Pasadena Mental Health Association and the Sherman Block Leadership Award from the California Peace Officers' Association. Melekian holds a bachelor's degree in American history and a master's degree in public administration from California State University, Northridge. He is a graduate of the 150th session of the FBI National Academy and the 20th class of the California Command College, where he was selected as class valedictorian. He is currently a Doctoral candidate in Public Policy at the University of Southern California.

Melekian served in the United States Army from 1967 to 1970. A member of the United States Coast Guard Reserve since 1984, he was called to active duty in 1991 during Operation Desert Storm. Melekian served a second tour of active duty in 2003 with the Coast Guard's Marine Safety and Security Team, in the Pacific area.

Richard W. (Rick) Myers has been chief of police in Colorado Springs, Colo. since January 2007. He previously served as chief of police for Appleton, Wis. since 1995, and before that as chief in Plymouth, Mich. and Lisle, Ill. He holds bachelor's and master's degrees in criminal justice from Michigan State University, and is a graduate of the FBI's National Academy, Law Enforcement Executive Development Seminar (LEEDS), and National Executive Institute. Chief Myers currently serves on the PERF Board of Directors as well as the board of commissioners of the Commission on Accreditation for Law Enforcement Agencies (CALEA). He is a past president of the Wisconsin Chiefs of Police Association, and a past president of Police Futurists International. Regarding his interest in the future of policing, Chief Myers recently made a presentation in which he forecast that police organizations may shift from a "pyramid" structure to a "matrix" or networked structure that will allow for easier exchanges of information, more flexibility, a greater ability to tolerate internal failures without large-scale damage, and greater effectiveness in dealing with decentralized crime or terrorist operations.

Robert K. Olson was appointed by the Irish Government to the newly created An Garda Siochana Inspectorate in 2006. The Inspectorate is tasked with evaluating the effectiveness of the 15,000-member Irish police force and recommending best international practices to the government. Prior to that, he spent 14 months in violence-torn Kingston, Jamaica as Chief of Party for PERF/USAID's Grants Pen Community Policing Project. Olson was appointed Chief of Police in Minneapolis in 1995 and served for nine years, retiring from active policing in 2004. Olson served as Police Commissioner in Yonkers, New York from 1990 to 1995 and as Chief of Police in Corpus Christi, Texas from 1987 through 1989. He started his policing career in Omaha, Neb. and rose through the ranks, becoming Deputy Chief of Police in 1982. Olson is a past board member and President of PERF as well as a longtime member of the Major Cities Chiefs Association, past member of state and county associations of chiefs of police in four states, and a life member of the International Association of Chiefs of Police. During his long policing career, Chief Olson has received numerous recognitions for his work, including PERF's Leadership Award and the Major Cities Chiefs' Bud Willoughby Award for Excellence in Police Administration. Chief Olson is a graduate of the University of Nebraska at Omaha with bachelor's and master's degrees in criminal justice. He is a graduate of the FBI's National Executive Institute and PERF's Senior Management Institute for Police. Olson is a Vietnam veteran, having served in the United States Army.

Kathleen O'Toole is the Chief Inspector of the Garda Síochána Inspectorate, an oversight body created by the Irish Government in 2005 to promote best practice, effectiveness and efficiency in Ireland's national police service. Earlier, she served on the Independent Commission on Policing in Northern Ireland (the "Patten Commission"), which led to the formation of the Police Service of Northern Ireland and reformed policing in that jurisdiction. O'Toole rose through the ranks of local and state police in Massachusetts. From 2004 to 2006, she was the first female Commissioner of the Boston Police Department. She also served as Massachusetts Secretary of Public Safety and as a Lieutenant Colonel in the Massachusetts State Police. She has held positions at Boston College and in various private-sector organizations, and founded an international consulting firm. She holds degrees from Boston College and the New England School of Law. She was admitted to the Massachusetts Bar in 1982.

Charles Ramsey was named Police Commissioner in Philadelphia in January 2008. Commissioner Ramsey previously served as the chief of the Metropolitan Police Department (MPD) of Washington, D.C. from 1998 to 2006. Under Chief Ramsey's leadership, the MPD regained its reputation as a national leader in policing. Crime rates declined 40 percent during his tenure, and community policing programs, hiring standards, training, equipment, facilities and fleet were dramatically upgraded. Furthermore, in the wake of a Pulitzer Prize-winning article in the *Washington Post* showing that MPD officers had shot and killed more people per capita than in any other big-city department, Ramsey asked the U.S. Justice Department to investigate and established reforms that resulted in a 63-percent reduction in officers' use of deadly force. Before taking the top police job in Washington, D.C., Chief Ramsey served in the Chicago Police Department for nearly three decades. He began his career there in 1968 as a police cadet and was promoted through the ranks. He was instrumental in designing and implementing the Chicago Alternative Policing Strategy (CAPS), a nationally acclaimed model of community policing. Commissioner Ramsey holds bachelor's and master's degrees in criminal justice from Lewis University, and is a graduate of the FBI National Academy and the FBI National Executive Institute. He has served as a member of the PERF board of directors and is a recipient of PERF's Gary P. Hayes award as well as the Leadership Award.

Darrel Stephens retired in 2008 as chief of the Charlotte-Mecklenburg, N.C. Police Department, a consolidated city-county department with more than 2,000 employees serving 713,000 people. His time as chief in Charlotte-Mecklenburg began in 1999, and before that he was chief in three other cities. He began his law enforcement career as a police officer, sergeant, and unit commander in Kansas City, Mo. He was assistant police chief in Lawrence, Kan. from 1976 to 1979, and then he was chief in Largo, Fla. until 1983. For the next three years, Stephens was chief in Newport News, Va., where he implemented an early community-oriented, problem-solving policing initiative. In 1986 he moved to Washington, D.C., where he served as PERF's executive director until 1992. Stephens then returned to running a police department, in St. Petersburg, Fla., where he served as chief for five years and then as city administrator for two more years, before taking the chief's position in Charlotte. Chief Stephens has a bachelor's degree in administration of justice from the University of Missouri-Kansas City and a master's degree in public administration from Central Missouri State University. In 2006 he received an honorary doctorate of laws degree from Central Missouri State University. He also has received PERF's highest honor, the Leadership Award.

John F. Timoney has been chief of police in Miami since 2003. A native of Dublin, Ireland, Timoney immigrated to the United States at the age of 13. He joined the New York City Police Department in 1967 and rapidly climbed through the ranks, culminating in his appointment in 1994 as the youngest-ever "four-star" chief of department in the city's history. A year later, he was named first deputy commissioner, which is the NYPD's second in command. He was widely credited with being one of the principal architects of the NYPD's successes in reducing crime in that period. Timoney also pursued higher education in New York, obtaining three degrees: a bachelor's degree from the John Jay College of Criminal Justice, a master's in American history from Fordham University, and a master's in urban planning from Hunter College. In 1998 Timoney was named police commissioner in Philadelphia, where he confronted serious problems. For example, the city's overburdened sex crimes unit was found to be burying hundreds of rape cases; cases went uninvestigated, and victims were not told that their complaints were being ignored. Timoney ordered a review of thousands of unsolved cases and undertook an unprecedented set of reforms. The result was that a sex crimes squad that was once among the nation's worst achieved a rate of solving rapes that distinguished itself as one of the best among large American cities. In Miami, Chief Timoney again took over a department mired in controversy over allegations of brutality and other problems, and he moved quickly to implement one of the most progressive policies in the nation on police use of deadly force, which brought a sharp reduction in the number of police shootings. He also has moved to improve police-community relations and ease racial tensions in the city. Timoney currently serves as President of PERF.

Ronnie Watson retired in 2007 as commissioner of police in Cambridge, Mass., completing a 44-year career in law enforcement. A Chicago native, Watson intended as a young man to become an accountant, but he came to the attention of Chicago Police Superintendent O.W. Wilson, who had been hired to clean up the Police Department following a scandal. Superintendent Wilson's reforms included aggressive recruitment of new officers, higher salaries to attract qualified officers, a strong merit system for promotions—and a new cadet program. In 1963, Ronnie Watson was one of the first 63 cadets chosen by Wilson. Watson worked in the Chicago Police Department for 33 years, rising through the ranks of sergeant, lieutenant, and captain, and commanding the gambling unit, the organized crime division, the training academy, and the Englewood district. He was instrumental in developing the Chicago Alternative Policing Strategy (CAPS), one of the most ambitious community policing programs in the United States. In 1996 Watson was chosen to head the Cambridge, Massachusetts Police Department. The number of homicides and other crimes in Cambridge dropped sharply during Commissioner Watson's tenure there, in part due to his innovations such as a Neighborhood Sergeants Program, which designates a sergeant to each of the city's 13 neighborhoods and makes each sergeant the "go-to" person for residents. The department also established a Visioning Project, which included surveying residents and police employees about their concerns and suggestions for improving policing in the city.

About the
Police Executive
Research Forum

The Police Executive Research Forum (PERF) is a professional organization of chief executives of city, county and state
law enforcement agencies who collectively serve more than
50 percent of the U.S. population. PERF's members include police
chiefs, superintendents, sheriffs, state police directors, university
police chiefs, public safety directors, and other law enforcement
professionals.

Established in 1976 as a nonprofit organization, PERF is committed to applying research to policing and to advancing profes-
sionalism in law enforcement. PERF also provides management
consulting and technical assistance to police agencies throughout
the world, and sponsors and conducts the Senior Management
Institute for Police (SMIP), a comprehensive management and
executive development training program for law enforcement
leaders.

PERF's success is built on the active involvement of its police
executive members. The organization also has types of membership that allow it to benefit from the diverse views of criminal justice researchers, law enforcement professionals of all ranks, and
others committed to improving policing services.

PERF has published some of the leading literature in the law
enforcement field, including reports on violent crime trends and
crime reduction strategies, community and problem-oriented
policing, the role of local police in enforcing federal immigration
laws, police use of force, police management of mass demonstra-
tions, terrorism in the local law enforcement context, racial profil-
ing, the police response to persons with mental illness, and other
critical issues.

To learn more about PERF, visit www.policeforum.org.

Appendix

Police Chief Compensation Packages

2009

Following are the results of a new survey of approximately 300 PERF-member police chiefs regarding salaries, benefits, and other aspects of their jobs.

Charlotte Lansinger, PERF's Executive Search consultant and one of the authors of PERF's book *Command Performance: Career Guide for Police Executives,* offered an analysis of this survey, including some comparisons with a similar survey that PERF conducted in1997.

Ms. Lansinger made the following points:

- The survey obtained a good nationwide cross-section of police agencies of all sizes, as measured in terms of employment levels and budgets.

- The highest salaries were found in Western states. Of the 27 chiefs who reported salaries of $175,000 or more, 21 were from Western states. And of course, higher salaries were found in larger departments.

- Salaries have increased; in 1997, almost half of the respondents made less than $85,000, but in the new survey, more than half of the responding chiefs reported salaries over $120,000.

- Little change was seen, compared to PERF's 1997 survey, in the length of service reported by responding chiefs. More than half of the responding chiefs in the new survey have been chief for 4 years or less.

- About 10 percent more chiefs reported having a contract in the new survey, compared to the 1997 survey.

- While only 4.6 percent of the responding chiefs in the new survey were female, that was an increase over the 1997 survey, when 0.6 percent of the chiefs were female.
- The average age of the responding chiefs seems to be increasing. In the 1997 survey, the highest frequency among the age brackets was in the 46-to-50 category; in the new survey, the highest frequency was found in the 51-to-55 bracket.
- Contracts for chief were most prevalent in the Northeast states, where 62 percent of chiefs reported having contracts, compared to the Midwest, South, and West, where majorities of respondents did *not* have contracts.
- There seems to be more rigidity among larger departments in the terms of their benefits packages. Compared to chiefs in smaller departments, fewer chiefs in large departments had customized benefits packages.
- There seems to be little correlation between whether a chief has a contract and whether the chief works for a mayor vs. a city manager type of government, or between the existence of a contract and the size of the police department.
- The size of the department, form of government, and region of the country also seem to have no correlation to the longevity of chiefs in their position.
- Regarding Question 9, only 42.1 percent of the responding chiefs reported that their benefits package includes liability insurance. "That number should be much higher," Lansinger said.
- Regarding pension plans (Question 10), nearly 57 percent of responding chiefs reported having a traditional "defined benefit" type of pension plan, where they are guaranteed a certain monthly annuity at a certain time of retirement. 18.8 percent had only a program like an IRA or 401(k), and 23.4 percent had a combination of both types of pension plans.

1. How many full-time staff does your agency employ?

Full-time sworn/commissioned	#	%
1–50	88	28.9
51–100	69	22.7
101–150	36	11.8
151–200	21	6.9
201–250	11	3.6
251–300	6	2.0
301–350	9	3.0
351–400	9	3.0
401–450	6	2.0
451–500	2	.7
501–1000	15	4.9
More than 1000	30	9.9
No answer	2	.7

Full-time non-sworn (civilian)	#	%
1–50	187	61.5
51–100	41	13.5
101–150	24	7.9
151–200	9	3.0
201–250	5	1.6
251–300	5	1.6
301–350	1	.3
351–400	4	1.3
More than 400	26	8.6
No answer	2	.7

2. What is your agency's overall annual budget for this fiscal year?

	#	%
Up to $1,000,000	10	3.3
$1,000,001 to $2,500,000	29	9.5
$2,500,001 to $5,000,000	36	11.8
$5,000,001 to $10,000,000	57	18.8
$10,000,001 to $20,000,000	58	19.1
$20,000,001 to $30,000,000	25	8.2
$30,000,001 to $40,000,000	10	3.3
$40,000,001 to $50,000,000	15	4.9
More than $50,000,000	56	18.4
No answer	8	2.6

3. What form of government does your city/county have? (mark one)

	#	%
City Manager	219	72.0
Mayor	65	21.4
Other	19	6.3
No answer	1	.3

4. What is your current annual base salary?

	#	%
Up to $50,000	1	0.3
$50,001 – $60,000	1	0.3
$60,001 – $65,000	2	0.7
$65,001 – $70,000	1	0.3
$70,001 – $75,000	5	1.6
$75,001 – $80,000	8	2.6
$80,001 – $85,000	7	2.3
$85,001 – $90,000	17	5.6
$90,001 – $95,000	12	3.9
$95,001 – $100,000	15	4.9
$100,001 – $120,000	72	23.7
More than $120,000	162	53.3
No answer	1	0.3

5. **What was your annual salary at the time of hire?**

	#	%
Up to $50,000	16	5.3
$50,001 – $60,000	10	3.3
$60,001 – $65,000	9	3.0
$65,001 – $70,000	12	3.9
$70,001 – $75,000	11	3.6
$75,001 – $80,000	20	6.6
$80,001 – $85,000	14	4.6
$85,001 – $90,000	23	7.6
$90,001 – $95,000	20	6.6
$95,001 – $100,000	26	8.6
$100,001 – $120,000	59	19.4
More than $120,000	72	23.7
No answer	12	3.9

6. **How long have you been the executive head of your agency?**

	#	%
Less than one year	26	8.6
1 year	43	14.1
2 years	37	12.2
3 years	31	10.2
4 years	35	11.5
5 years	24	7.9
6 years	19	6.3
7 years	20	6.6
8 years	14	4.6
9 years	8	2.6
10 years	10	3.3
11–15 years	19	6.3
16–20 years	14	4.6
More than 20 years	4	1.3

7. Do you have a contract or employment agreement?

	#	%
Yes	110	36.2
No	193	63.5
No answer	1	0.3

7b. If "yes", does your contract have a severance agreement?

Yes	72	65.5
No	35	31.8
No answer	3	2.7

8. Is your benefits package: (mark one)

	#	%
The standard employee benefits package	219	72.0
A customized benefits package	84	27.6
No answer	1	0.3

9. Does your benefits package include any of the following? (mark all that apply)

	#	%
Health insurance	283	93.1
Professional liability insurance	128	42.1
Dental insurance	253	83.2
Deferred retirement (non-contributory)	135	44.4
Deferred compensation (contributory)	190	62.5
Life insurance	260	85.5
Vision care insurance	195	64.1
Compensatory time	91	29.9
Other	86	28.3

10. Please select the scenario that most closely describes how your retirement contributions are made and benefits received.

	#	%
Defined benefit plan (employer funded plan which guarantees a specific monthly benefit at retirement)	173	56.9
Choose one:		
a. State plan	117	67.6
b. Local plan	45	26.0
c. Both	10	5.8
d. Not Applicable/No answer	1	0.6
Defined contribution plan (employee and/or employer contributes to your individual account– often a 401(k) or IRA–employee contributions are invested as pre-tax deductions and, at retirement, you receive the balance of your account)	57	18.8
Both defined benefit and contribution plan	71	23.4
No answer	3	1.0

11. Is your pension program portable?

	#	%
Yes	187	61.5
No	110	36.2
Not applicable/No answer	7	2.3

11a. If "yes", is it portable out of state?

Yes	40	21.4
No	137	73.3
Not applicable/No answer	10	5.3

12. Are you eligible for incentive bonuses?

	#	%
Yes	81	26.6
No	220	72.4
No answer	3	1.0

12a. If "yes", are they tied to specific performance measures?

	#	%
Yes	52	64.2
No	29	35.8

13. Are you reimbursed for any of the following expenses? (mark all that apply)

	#	%
Membership fees for professional organizations	279	91.8
Travel expenses for professional conferences	289	95.1
Business related lunch/dinner meetings	216	71.1
Professional subscriptions	262	86.2
Moving expenses when hired	137	45.1
Executive development programs	237	78.0
House hunting trips	38	12.5
Temporary living quarters	43	14.1
Other	16	5.3

14. What provisions have been made for your business automobile? (mark all that apply)

	#	%
Automobile included in benefits package	135	44.4
Employer leases vehicle; employer selects make	6	2.0
Employer leases vehicle; employee selects make	7	2.3
May use employer-owned vehicle for business use only	72	23.7
May use employer-owned vehicle for business and personal use	147	48.4
Other	29	9.5

15. What is your race?

	#	%
Asian	3	1.0
Caucasian	267	87.8
Hispanic	13	4.3
African American	15	4.9
Pacific Islander	1	.3
Native American	1	.3
Other	4	1.3

16. What is your gender?

	#	%
Male	290	95.4
Female	14	4.6

17. What is your age?

	#	%
40 or younger	3	1.0
41–45	26	8.6
46–50	71	23.4
51–55	107	35.2
56–60	71	23.4
61–65	22	7.2
Over 65	4	1.3

18. What is the highest level of education you have obtained?

	#	%
Bachelor's Degree	85	28.0
Master's Degree	201	66.1
Law Degree	9	3.0
Ph.D.	8	2.6
Other	1	0.3

19. What is the population of the jurisdiction in which you serve?

	#	%
Up to 50,000	137	45.1
50,001 – 75,000	46	15.1
75,001 – 100,000	19	6.3
100,001 – 150,000	24	7.9
150,001 – 200,000	12	3.9
200,001 – 250,000	13	4.3
250,001 – 300,000	5	1.6
300,001 – 500,000	16	5.3
500,001 – 1,000,000	18	5.9
More than 1,000,000	13	4.3
No answer	1	.3